Attention Deficit Disorder

Attention Deficit Disorder

ADHD and ADD Syndromes

SECOND EDITION

DALE R. JORDAN

pro·ed
8700 Shoal Creek Boulevard
Austin, Texas 78757

Printed in the United States of America

Library of Congress Cataloging-in-Publication Data

Jordan, Dale R.
    Attention deficit disorder : ADHD and ADD syndromes / Dale R.
Jordan. — 2nd ed.
      p.   cm.
    Includes bibliographical references
    ISBN 0-89079-530-4
    1. Attention-deficit hyperactivity disorder. I. Title.
    [DNLM: 1. Attention Deficit Disorder with Hyperactivity. WS
350.6 J76a]
    RJ506.H9J67 1992
    618.92′8589—dc20
    DNLM/DLC
    for Library of Congress   92-3217
                                      CIP

pro·ed

8700 Shoal Creek Boulevard
Austin, Texas 78757

3 4 5 6 7 8 9 10   98 97 96 95 94

To Martha
For 39 years
my extraordinary wife
whose patience and wisdom
have enabled me to become
what I am today.

Contents

Preface

*In a time of drastic change, it is the learners
who inherit the future. The learned usually
find themselves equipped to live in a world
that no longer exists.* (Hoffer, 1982, p. 83)

The concept of attention deficit disorder is pressing educators, counselors, and parents hard. It is difficult to comprehend how bright persons, both children and adults, can continue to be as immature as others several years below their age. The clearly visible patterns we now call attention deficit–hyperactivity disorder (ADHD) and the largely invisible problem we call attention deficit disorder without hyperactivity (ADD) challenge many of the concepts held for generations by professionals. We cannot meet this new challenge by clinging to old ideas or attitudes. Seeing the multiple manifestations of attention deficit disorder calls for new eyes. Dealing with it successfully requires new levels of compassion and flexibility. Those who are not open to new knowledge may, as Hoffer implied, find themselves living in a diagnostic and therapeutic world that no longer meets the needs of this special population. It is my hope that this discussion of attention deficit disorder will stimulate creative thinking in how to be more successful in treating these often hyperactive, frequently passive strugglers.

Dale R. Jordan, Ph.D.
Jones Learning Center
University of the Ozarks
Clarksville, AR 72830

FORMS OF ATTENTION DEFICIT DISORDER

I n 1985, a rather astonishing fact was reported in the *Mental Health Letter* published by the Harvard Medical School: Almost half of all childhood referrals made to mental health agencies are for attention deficit disorder. Before the 1980s, other labels had been used for this frequent problem: minimal brain dysfunction (MBD), hyperactivity, hyperkinesis, learning disability, short attention span, and immaturity. During the rapid changes in the American culture following World War II, educators began to describe the inattentive child in the classroom. During the 1950s, it seemed that our schools were filling up with youngsters who did not or could not pay attention. Educators began to focus upon students who were too easily distractible, could not tune out the edges and concentrate on the middle of their environment, could not follow a series of instructions without being reminded, and could not fit successfully into a group. Distractibility and short attention span became prominent topics at meetings where school leaders discussed their frustrations.

The concept of minimal brain dysfunction was born during the 1960s, largely because of the influence of a psychologist, Samuel Clements (1966). MBD referred to a certain type of child who listened poorly, remembered details poorly, could not follow through without supervision, quickly forgot what was learned, became overly frustrated too easily, could not tolerate normal classroom pressure, and was hyperactive. Skill development in the basic subjects of reading, phonics, spelling, math, and language was spotty and unpredictable. What this child knew on Tuesday was likely forgotten or confused by Wednesday. These children were overly irritable under stress that was normally absorbed by their agemates. Youngsters with MBD symptoms were impulsive and often destructive, having no sense of how to handle things gently. They were compulsive and demanding in a self-centered way, clamoring to satisfy whims of the moment. They were dubbed the "now children," demanding that wishes be satisfied now, not later. They were hyperactive, impulsive, compulsive, irritable, poorly organized, self-centered youngsters who were often medicated by cortical stimulants, such as Ritalin™, which frequently reduced their behavior to "normal" levels.

This concept of MBD answered an important question of the 1960s. It helped educators understand that certain underachievers were neurologically different, and that this physical difference was the cause of such irregular behavior. Children with MBD patterns were regarded as a special population who needed special treatment within the educational arena. They could not be incorporated successfully into traditional classrooms where standard materials and methodology were used. These youngsters must be handled differently because they *were* different. This model of MBD played a major part in the development of special education programs during the late 1960s and 1970s. Students who had MBD patterns were placed in self-contained classrooms that were largely isolated from the mainstream educational program. It was often assumed that a child with MBD patterns would always be that way to a large degree. In the 1960s and 1970s, the purpose of special education was not to change the child, but to help the handicapped student get ready to cope with the world in years to come.

In this isolated environment where learning specialists could interact more intensely with struggling learners, a significant pattern began to be seen. By the late 1970s, it was recognized that not all children who displayed the MBD pattern were hyperactive. The earmark of hyperactivity did not apply to all of the underachievers who had poor listening ability, short retention of learned information, and low tolerance for stress. It became apparent that being hyperactive was not a reliable criterion for identifying a child with MBD. It also became apparent that at certain age levels, some of these strugglers began to change. Over a period of time, skill development increased remarkably in many students with MBD, along with increased social success. As these children entered puberty, the original cluster of learning disability symptoms began to disappear. Educators realized that a new point of view must be developed to account for those children with minimal brain dysfunction who were not hyperactive and who began to outgrow most of their learning struggles at a certain point.

For many years, the point of reference in clinical diagnosis of mental and emotional problems has been the *Diagnostic and Statistical Manual of Mental Disorders* (DSM) of the American Psychiatric Association (APA). During the late 1970s, APA began revising the clinical definitions and categories of mental and emotional illness for a third edition of the *Diagnostic and Statistical Manual of Mental Disorders.* When DSM-III was published in February 1980, a fundamental change was presented in how clinicians could interpret behavior patterns related to short attention and inability to maintain integrated thought patterns. Instead of the old umbrella concept of minimal brain dysfunction, the 1980 APA definitions provided three categories for interpreting the underachiever:

314.01 Attention Deficit Disorder with Hyperactivity

314.00 Attention Deficit Disorder without Hyperactivity

314.80 Attention Deficit Disorder, Residual Type

Suddenly those involved with educating the underachiever had a new model for interpreting this academic and behavioral problem. Some underachievers were hyperactive; many were not. Most underachievers would gradually outgrow much of the syndrome; some would not. During the developmental years of adolescence, most children with attention deficit disorder would progressively overcome much of the problem if certain kinds of help were provided; however, some would not. Some children with attention deficit disorder would become adults who had not outgrown the patterns that complicated their early years so much. This change in diagnostic point of view became a critical factor in recognizing the prevalence of neurologically based learning problems in the classroom.

The search for understanding of attention deficit disorder has been something like Captain Ahab seeking the great white whale. A persistent school of thought within the diagnostic community insists that to be a white whale (to have attention deficit disorder), the creature must thrash about, create constant motion, and be hyperactive. If something that looks like a white whale is quiet, passive, and just floats along, it cannot therefore be a white whale. According to this point of view, objects in the sea might have the size and appearance of the sought-after great white whale, but if the beast is not hyperactive, it cannot be considered by the hunter. No matter how many passive whalelike creatures float by Captain Ahab's boat, he must discount everything that does not kick up waves of activity and blow clouds of steam over the water.

A similar point of view seems to have prevailed among specialists who decided upon the definitions of behavior patterns included in the APA *Diagnostic and Statistical Manual*. In 1987, a major revision of the DSM-III was published. In the 1987 DSM-III-R, the three earlier categories of attention deficit disorder were replaced by only one category under the label of attention deficit–hyperactivity disorder (DSM-III-R, 314.01). This diagnostic category presents 14 possible symptoms of attention deficit–hyperactivity disorder (ADHD). A person must show 8 of the 14 symptoms to be identified clinically as having ADHD. Ironically, only 5 of the 14 symptoms within this list relate to hyperactivity as such. Diagnosticians continually face the dilemma of having to explain how a passive, nonhyperactive child who cannot keep his or her attention focused is categorized as "hyperactive." However, because the DSM-III-R is the primary authority for authorizing insurance coverage for treatment of ADHD or attention deficit disorder without hyperactivity (ADD), clinicians have no choice but to use this code book. It is extremely awkward for specialists to justify nonhyperactive forms of attention deficit based on the way the 1987 diagnostic codes are presented.

The DSM-III-R does include a category called undifferentiated attention deficit disorder (UADD), with the code number 314.00. Some of the patterns described in DSM-III under code 314.00, attention deficit disorder without hyperactivity, are found here. However, this category in the DSM-III-R is ambivalent and unclear. Diagnosticians face the predicament of dealing with patterns of nonhyperactive attention deficits without a clear clinical description of those patterns. As we shall see in this chapter, students who have passive attention deficit patterns are overlooked according to the DSM-III-R nomenclature (Jordan, 1991).

It is difficult to find an explanation for this lack of clarity in the DSM-III-R position on attention deficit disorders. Some specialists explain that the 1987 changes were necessary to conform to the international diagnostic codes that do not recognize nonhyperactive patterns of attention deficit disorders (Silver, 1991). Others insist that not enough research has been done to establish ADD (without hyperactivity) as a clearly seen syndrome. To complicate diagnostic matters further, a newer edition of the *Diagnostic and Statistical Manual* will be published during the 1990s. Many professionals hope that DSM-IV will restore the category of attention deficit disorder without hyperactivity as a clearly defined syndrome. Meanwhile, professionals and parents must do the best they can with the unclear guidelines created by the DSM-III-R.

For the remainder of this book, two designations of attention deficit are used. ADHD stands for attention deficit–hyperactivity disorder, and ADD stands for attention deficit disorder without hyperactivity. As we shall see, ADD does indeed exist, with often devastating results at home, at school, and on the job.

ADHD and ADD are often complicated by other kinds of learning or behavior problems that affect the way these students handle new information. Many persons who have ADHD or ADD are also dyslexic (Copeland, 1991; Hagerman, 1983; Jordan, 1988, 1989; Wender, 1987). Not only are their thought patterns loose and poorly organized, but they tend to reverse symbols, scramble information that goes in a certain sequence, have poor memory for spelling, and stumble over reading. Students who have ADHD or ADD often have poor eye muscle coordination that interferes with accurate focusing of both eyes as a team (Jordan, 1988, 1989). Late physical maturity is common, which causes social problems and difficulty fitting into groups of peers (Jordan, 1989). Persons who have ADHD are often allergic to certain food substances. These cytotoxic elements in the diet send them into orbit with extreme hyperactive reactions triggered by what they eat or drink (Crook, 1990; Hagerman, 1983; Powers, 1976; Taylor, 1990; von Hilshimer, 1974; Wunderlich, 1973). Few persons who have ADHD or ADD have only one specific problem. Multiple factors usually must be taken into account to work with these students successfully.

Various professional opinions exist as to what causes ADHD or ADD. It now appears that ADHD and ADD are inherited and are caused by physical differences within the brain (Anastopoulos & Barkley, 1991). Most children with these problems have relatives with similar patterns. Biochemical research and brain imaging have revealed that the chemistry of the brain is different in persons who have attention deficits. The myelin sheath surrounding nerve tissues within the normal brain seems to be delayed in reaching full maturity in these persons. The nerve pathways within the brain are therefore unable to function in a mature way. Thought patterns and mental images are mixed and incomplete because the physical construction of the brain is immature and different.

In 1990, Alan Zametkin and colleagues reported results of positron emission tomography (PET) brain imaging studies of children and adults who have ADHD (see also Zametkin, 1991). Zametkin et al. found that three areas of the left brain in persons with ADHD patterns fail to use sugar (brain glucose) fast enough to maintain normal thought patterns and muscle response (see Figure 1.1). This irregular metabolism of brain sugar triggers certain ADHD behavior patterns, which interfere with classroom performance, social skills, and job performance in some children and adults.

In 1991, Martha Denckla reported results from a different kind of brain imaging study of children with ADHD and ADD. Magnetic resonance imaging (MRI) research at the Johns Hopkins School of Medicine has revealed immature, incomplete functions within the cerebellum. This deficit in cerebellar function triggers such problems as poor organization and poor inhibition of impulses. The result is behavior that is never well organized and is usually impulsive.

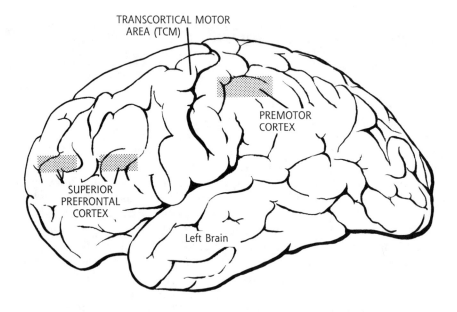

FIGURE 1.1. Areas of the left brain where sugar usage (brain glucose metabolism) is lower in persons who have ADHD than in those who do not have ADHD patterns. (Based upon the model reported by Alan Zametkin et al., 1990.)

Attention Deficit–Hyperactivity Disorder (ADHD)

The most obvious form of attention deficit disorder is the hyperactive form (DSM-III-R, 314.00). No one who deals with a hyperactive, poorly organized child misses the fact that something is wrong. Yet it appears that no more than half of all children with attention deficits are hyperactive (Hagerman, 1983; Jordan, 1988, 1989, 1991). Because most persons who have ADHD are above average in intelligence, mental age is usually far ahead of social maturity and the ability to carry out responsibility. The hyperactive person with loose thought patterns is usually bright; however, the person's good intelligence is not available for organized use. The following sections describe behavior patterns that are earmarks of attention deficit–hyperactivity disorder (ADHD).

Short Attention

The child who has ADHD cannot hold full attention on any formal task for more than a few seconds at a time. As the child listens to new information or receives a set of instructions, attention begins to break down. Within a short time, the child's attention has become fixed upon something else. The youngster who has ADHD is like a mosquito, zipping about the environment, flitting rapidly from one point of attention to another. Ray Wunderlich (1973) described these youngsters as being like bullets that "ricochet" off the environment. It is impossible for these children to maintain full attention long enough to do what adults expect. Thought patterns are too loose and too poorly organized for the children to concentrate on the same issue long enough to finish a task.

Easily Distracted

It is impossible for the child who has ADHD to ignore what goes on nearby. The attention darts to nearby movement to see what is going on. The child's attention leaps toward any sound to find out what is happening. An unusual odor is an irresistible attraction, and the child must see where the smell is coming from. A change in temperature or an unexpected puff of air captures the attention, jerking it away from the main responsibility. Pressure of clothing demands immediate satisfaction, with a lot of scratching and tugging at garments to relieve the sensation. Moments of skin itch become the main point of concern, and the itch must be scratched. Feelings within the body as gas bubbles work through the abdominal area or a belch erupts cannot be ignored. Any change, anything new or different in the child's environment, calls for immediate investigation. Children who have ADHD cannot ignore these intrusions into their sensory awareness.

Poor Listening

Youngsters who have ADHD cannot stay on track in listening. When a flow of oral information comes their way, they cannot absorb the full message. Only bits and pieces of what they hear remain firmly fixed in the memory. When the listening experience is over, the child clamors, "What? What did you say?" There is no retention of what was just explained or described. Most students who have ADHD fully understand only part of what they hear at school or home. As a rule, less than 30% of the full oral message is absorbed and retained (Jordan, 1988, 1989, 1991). Later these students exclaim, "You didn't tell me that!" or "I didn't hear you say that!" Comprehending a stream of oral information is exceedingly poor for these youngsters.

Unfinished Business

Children who have ADHD do not finish what they start. No task is completed unless a great deal of supervision and reminding is done by adults.

On his or her own, the child starts many projects but finishes none. Only part of a work page was completed, yet the child is certain that all of it was done. Only part of the material was copied from the board, but the child is convinced that all of it was copied. For instance, the student who has ADHD often begins a math assignment, but soon loses attention and begins to skip over problems or misread the math signs. These students then become so frustrated they stop trying. They usually turn in incomplete papers thinking they have finished all of the work. Figures 1.2, 1.3, and 1.4 show examples of unfinished math assignments.

Children who have ADHD are constantly losing things. Homework assignments that were completed under parents' supervision are lost before they reach school the next day. Books, pencils, and workbooks disappear from the student's workspace or locker. Jackets, caps, and play equipment vanish. Teeth are only partly brushed. Hair is only partly shampooed. Baths are left unfinished. Chores are started but not completed. Children who have ADHD are too scattered to go from start to finish without firm supervision.

Impulsivity

The child who has ADHD does not think ahead. There is no postponing a wish or desire. The child demands it *now*. He or she wants it *now*. No thought is given as to what the effect will be if the impulse is satisfied at this moment. The impulsive child has tunnel vision, seeing only what

$$\begin{array}{cccccc}
\begin{array}{r} 1 \\ +3 \\ \hline 4 \end{array} &
\begin{array}{r} 5 \\ +4 \\ \hline 9 \end{array} &
\begin{array}{r} 47 \\ +\ 2 \\ \hline \end{array} &
\begin{array}{r} 7 \\ +9 \\ \hline 14 \end{array} &
\begin{array}{r} 66 \\ +\ 4 \\ \hline \end{array} &
\begin{array}{r} 86 \\ +29 \\ \hline 113 \end{array}
\end{array}$$

FIGURE 1.2. Math assignment of a 14-year-old boy who has ADHD. Although he intended to finish the addition problems when he skipped them, he became distracted and failed to do so. He turned in his paper thinking that he had finished the assignment.

$$\begin{array}{cccccc}
\begin{array}{r} 5 \\ -3 \\ \hline 2 \end{array} &
\begin{array}{r} 8 \\ -2 \\ \hline 6 \end{array} &
\begin{array}{r} 76 \\ -12 \\ \hline 64 \end{array} &
\begin{array}{r} 14 \\ -\ 6 \\ \hline 12 \end{array} &
\begin{array}{r} 25 \\ -16 \\ \hline 11 \end{array} &
\begin{array}{r} 370 \\ -\ 82 \\ \hline 312 \end{array}
\end{array}$$

FIGURE 1.3. Math work of a 10-year-old girl who has ADHD. She began to subtract, and then became distracted. When she returned to her work, she did not notice the subtraction signs. By this time, she was too confused and disorganized to think clearly. To fill the answer spaces, she partly added and partly subtracted the remaining problems.

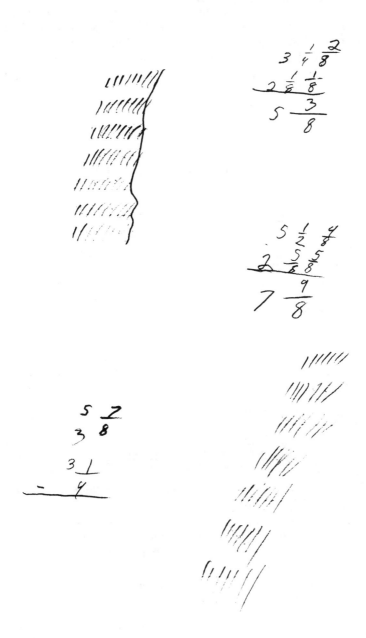

FIGURE 1.4. Math work of a 14-year-old boy who has ADHD. This student cannot maintain organized mental images to work fractions. He tries to keep track by marking "counters" on his paper. Then he becomes too confused as he counts the marks, so he gives up trying to finish his assignment.

he or she wants now. Everything else is shut out of consideration. The child does not recognize how satisfying the impulse now will affect or inconvenience others. No notice is given to possible destruction that might occur in satisfying the desire of the moment. Children who have ADHD who bump and knock things around simply do not realize what they are doing to their environment. They do not connect the consequences with the action.

Poor Organization

It is impossible for the child who has ADHD to organize. The ingredients of the situation do not come together into an organized whole. This child does not see a cluttered room with things tossed every which way. He or she locks in on only a few of the items and does not see the rest. The child is bewildered when adults demand that "this mess must be cleaned up." The child who has ADHD does not see a mess. Teachers demand that the desk be kept in a more orderly way, but the child does not see a state of disorder. The parts do not connect within the child's mental image to form a whole. The concept of organization does not exist for most youngsters who have ADHD unless it is imposed by someone from the outside.

Disruptiveness

Because the child with ADHD does not plug into his or her whole environment, there is no awareness of the usual social amenities. When a thought comes to mind, the child blurts it out. When an itch occurs, the child scratches noisily. When things need to be moved, the child does so loudly with exaggerated motions and commotion. When turns must be taken, the child bursts ahead of others. When things must be shared, the child grabs instead of waiting. The child who has ADHD is noisy, intrusive, and insensitive to the rights of others. He or she does not see the space markers that help any group maintain good order. The child barges in without noticing that he or she should stay out. He or she reaches into another person's territory without paying attention to the signals that he or she is not welcome. The child who has ADHD does not see the usual courteous ways of fitting into a group. Any group activity is disrupted by impulsive, spontaneous behavior that is seldom self-contained. This child puts a great deal of pressure upon those who must share his or her space.

Body Energy Overflow

The body of a child who has ADHD is never completely at rest. Motor signals that tell muscles to work continually overflow. Feet scrub the floor.

Legs drum the sides of the desk. Hands roam the area finding things to handle. Bodies thrash about in chairs. Loud sighs and vocal noises emerge inadvertently. Pencils clack against the desk top. Books topple with a thud to the floor. Paper is ripped from a tablet with too much force. The whole body may begin to rock in an overflow rhythm that causes the chair to squeak or grind. The body of a student who has ADHD cannot be still longer than brief periods of time. It is impossible for the child to stop the energy overflow. If gum chewing is permitted, the child smacks and slurps. If snacks are served, food is spilled on the table and floor. If quiet time is supposed to be observed, the child is up and out of the chair several times. The body is in some kind of motion most of the time, even during sleep. The next morning the bed looks like it hosted a wrestling match during the night. This kinetic overflow is inadvertent, usually beyond the conscious will of the child who has ADHD.

Emotional Overflow

The child who has ADHD does not fit successfully into groups. He or she almost never is a successful member of a class. The child is much less mature than most peers. Academic skills are usually behind schedule, leaving the child unable to compete or earn praise. More mature classmates complain that he or she "acts like a baby" because of uncontrolled floods of emotion. Outbursts of anger are common and, over a period of time, explosions involving tears occur frequently. When the child is compared with classmates who are learning new skills on schedule, he or she is seen as immature, irritable, disruptive, demanding, and uncooperative. The group soon becomes tired of this pattern and rejects the child, who ends up outside the group as an outcast. Being a misfit is one of the usual plights of the student who has ADHD.

Insatiability

An earmark of many children who have ADHD is insatiability. Cravings are never fully satisfied. Enough is never obtained. Attention from the teacher or parent is never as much as the child needs or wants. Playmates become exhausted from constant demands for more. There is an irrational component in these insatiable demands. The child does not respond to commonsense reasoning. He or she does not understand when the adult says, "You have had enough." The demand is for more. The clamor is, "Let's do it again." The cry is, "He got a bigger piece than I got." The child is a pain to take shopping because he or she clamors for everything in the store. This child tends to be jealous, accusing others of not giving him or her a fair share. In the family, this child accuses parents of loving others more. The emotional needs of the child who has ADHD can be a bottomless pit that cannot be filled. No matter how much love and affection are bestowed, it is not enough. The child whines and badgers and pleads for more.

Blame of Others

Because the child who has ADHD does not perceive the whole but deals only with disorganized parts, he or she does not see the normal chain of cause and effect. There is no organized perception of what caused an event to take place. It is always the fault of someone else. The cat broke the vase, or the neighbor broke the window. Sister Ann made the mess in the kitchen, or brother Mario left the towels on the bathroom floor. Mom made the child late to school. The teacher did not explain the assignment to the class. The bell rang too early for books to be found in the locker. The prices were too high at the store, so that is why all of the allowance was gone the second day. Blame of others is often a complicating factor when dealing with the youngster who has ADHD.

Overreaction to Criticism

It is almost impossible for the person who has ADHD to handle constructive criticism. The child does not see the purpose of the criticism. He or she locks in on only the sound of the words, the tone of the adult's voice, or the red marks on the paper. This oversensitivity often leads to a paranoid attitude in later years. The child who has ADHD has unrealistic expectations, confidently expecting that the next task will be done well. When it is left unfinished, or when important items are omitted, the child bursts into self-defense rather than hearing what the critic has to say. It is difficult for leaders to handle this oversensitivity successfully.

Chronic Make-Believe

A prevalent pattern in children who have ADHD is almost constant make-believe. On the one hand, this tendency to fantasize is the child's way of handling life that is otherwise intolerable. Chronic make-believe often takes the form of acting out feelings through another object, such as a doll or stuffed toy animal. By pretending that it is the doll or stuffed toy speaking, the child who has ADHD verbalizes and acts out intense feelings of anger, frustration, and fear. By having the doll or stuffed animal have a tantrum, the child who has ADHD can avoid being punished. The vicarious game of having the make-believe partner have the tantrum, say angry words to others, break things, disobey rules, or utter unacceptable language allows the child who has ADHD to face indirectly the strong emotions he or she is feeling.

On the other hand, children who have ADHD often become so deeply habituated to this kind of make-believe that they lose sight of the boundary between reality and fantasy. It often becomes impossible for them to stop their chronic make-believe habits. These children act out a great deal of pain, anger, frustration, disappointment, and hostility by channeling it through their make-believe partners. Adults usually do not punish the child when it is clear that the make-believe partner did the deed or said the unacceptable words. This form of make-believe takes the child who has ADHD close to the thin line that divides healthy thinking from neurotic thinking. Chronic make-believe carries many of these struggling youngsters safely through difficult years when life threatens to overwhelm the child because of constant inability to handle life successfully. Occasionally, an overly sensitive child slips over the edge of reality into a strongly neurotic state through the use of chronic make-believe.

Attention Deficit Disorder Without Hyperactivity (ADD)

Earlier in this chapter, we considered the metaphor of Captain Ahab searching for the hyperactive great white whale, which certainly does exist in the ocean of human behavior. We described Captain Ahab's point of view that causes him not to recognize the passive, quiet white whales that float everywhere around his boat. The problem with Captain Ahab's restricted point of view is that he does not recognize that at least half of those passive, quiet whalelike creatures are indeed white whales. They float along not making waves or blowing clouds of steam, yet they are there in every direction. In the classroom, many of our struggling learners are quiet and passive, and do not attract attention to themselves the way hyperactive classmates advertise their struggle. At least half of all students who have attention deficits appear *not* to be hyperactive (Hagerman, 1983; Jordan, 1988, 1989, 1991). The following sections describe behavior patterns that are earmarks of attention deficit disorder without hyperactivity, often called ADD (Copeland, 1991; Jordan, 1988, 1989, 1991; Wender, 1987). The fact that Captain Ahab does not use this label does not mean that it does not exist.

Drifting Away from the Task

The child who has ADHD darts off on rabbit trails, kicking up disruptive dust that attracts everyone's attention. The passive child who has ADD drifts away quietly. A casual observer sees no telltale signs that the mind has wandered. A close observer sees a faraway look in the eyes as if the child is off in another world, but the child's body is usually still. This quiet drifter can float for long periods of time, not learning new material or absorbing new knowledge, before adults are aware of the problem. These children are often called stargazers or daydreamers. No matter how hard they try to stay on task, their attention drifts away. Thought patterns are too loose to let them hold onto their first mental images over a period of time.

Loose Thought Patterns

It is impossible for children who have ADD to maintain tight, well-organized thought patterns. Information in sequence becomes cluttered and scrambled. Important pieces of information drop out, leaving gaps in the mental image. Steps that should be followed in a certain order become scrambled and mixed together. Information that has been learned does not appear on the "mental screen" when it is needed. New information does not become connected or integrated with what has already been learned. Memory patterns are too loose to let the student do groups of things well. For example, several spelling words may be written correctly; then the student misses the next several words in the list. The first few math problems may be worked correctly, then he or she starts to make mistakes in the next several problems. There is a "short circuit" quality in the way the child thinks, remembers, and analyzes.

Figure 1.5 shows the work of a bright high school student who has ADD. No matter how hard he tries, he cannot go from start to finish in assignments, especially math. He quickly reaches mental burnout and can no longer keep on thinking about his task. He is a quiet, passive person who does not attract attention to himself. Teachers often do not realize when he has lost track and needs help coming back to his task.

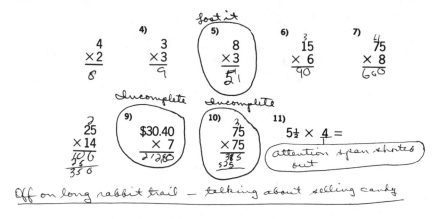

FIGURE 1.5. Math work of a 15-year-old boy with ADD. Because of his very slow processing speed, this student needs three to four times longer than normal to finish assignments. He becomes lost, drifts off onto mental rabbit trails without being aware that he has done so. He begins daydreaming and talking about other things instead of staying on task. He needs continual supervision to finish what he is supposed to do.

Students who have ADD often experience short circuit thinking as they do assignments. For a while, they have clear mental images; then they begin to "short out" in frequent cycles. They start to make mistakes even when they know the material well. They they catch themselves, get the next few items correctly, then begin making mistakes again. When they reach the point of mental burnout, they can no longer recognize their errors or correct them without help. Figure 1.6 shows this pattern in the

FIGURE 1.6. Spelling test of a 16-year-old girl who has ADD. She is an excellent reader for brief periods of time, and she has no other types of learning difficulties. She knows spelling rules when someone keeps her attention focused. On her own during a spelling test, she cannot hold her attention focused long enough to pull all of her knowledge together without being reminded.

spelling test of a 16-year-old high school student who has ADD. When someone calls her attention to her mistakes, she has no trouble correcting the spelling errors; however, she often cannot do so on her own.

Students who have ADD often do not reach mental burnout until after they have worked for several minutes. However, when they do reach the point of burnout, mistakes begin to flood their work. Figure 1.7 shows the work of an intelligent high school student with this delayed burnout pattern.

Shift of First Impressions

Children who have ADD do not hold onto first impressions. In sounding out words, the first impression may be correct, then it changes within the child's mind, causing the first impression to seem wrong. The child spends a great deal of work time erasing and changing what was written first. Math problems that were correct suddenly seem incorrect. Impressions of what is seen and heard do not stay together. Soon the child is confused by the jumbled impressions that at first seemed clear and accurate. It takes these children a long time to finish written assignments. More time is spent erasing and changing than doing the work itself. Oral answers are constantly changed, usually before the child has finished speaking his or her first thoughts. Multiple-choice tests are agonizing because the student constantly goes back to change first responses. True–false tests often drive these students to tears because they cannot settle on a best choice. This shift of first impressions causes these students to split hairs over every issue, then they split the splits. This constant change of first impressions eats up their work time, causing them always to be behind schedule in finishing assignments and tests.

Figure 1.8 shows the work of a 7-year-old girl who has ADD. Her written work is filled with "shadows" of first writing that was erased and changed. It is impossible for her to keep up with classmates in writing assignments. She takes much unfinished work home to be completed at night.

Time Lag

The central nervous system of children who have ADD often does not deliver needed information on schedule. It is not unusual for many seconds or several minutes to go by before a full mental image is developed. These children spend long periods of time pondering, searching the memory, and trying it several different ways. It is impossible for them to speed up the rate at which the central nervous system processes information. They have no choice but to sit and wait. As they wait, they tend to drift, which greatly complicates performance problems. These students often whisper over and over to themselves, quietly rehearsing until all of the

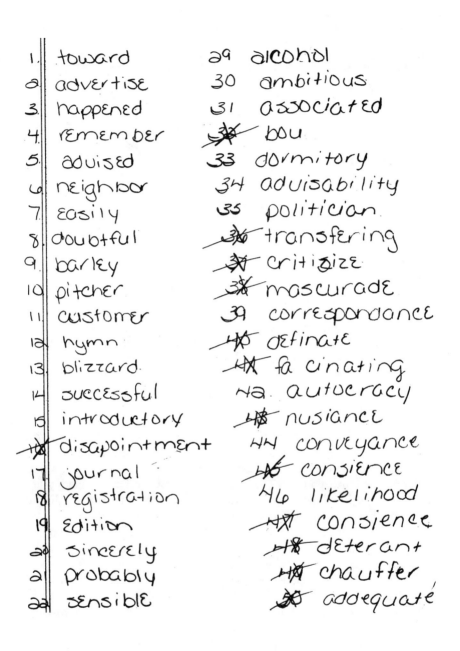

1. toward
2. advertise
3. happened
4. remember
5. advised
6. neighbor
7. easily
8. doubtful
9. barley
10. pitcher
11. customer
12. hymn
13. blizzard
14. successful
15. introductory
16. ~~disapointment~~
17. journal
18. registration
19. edition
20. sincerely
21. probably
22. sensible

29. alcohol
30. ambitious
31. associated
32. ~~bou~~
33. dormitory
34. advisability
35. politician
36. ~~transfering~~
37. ~~critizize~~
38. ~~mascurade~~
39. correspondance
40. ~~definate~~
41. ~~fa cinating~~
42. autocracy
43. ~~nusiance~~
44. conveyance
45. ~~consience~~
46. likelihood
~~consience~~
~~deterant~~
~~chauffer~~
~~addequate~~

FIGURE 1.7. Spelling test of a 15-year-old boy who has ADD. The student's mental images hold together for several minutes, allowing him to remember spelling patterns clearly. Then attention burnout begins, and he becomes mentally disorganized. As this burnout process starts, he no longer can focus his attention on spelling patterns that he actually knows.

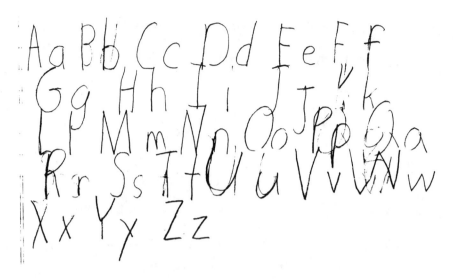

FIGURE 1.8.   Work of a 7-year-old girl who has ADD. She is continually criticized for "messy writing." Every paper is filled with erasures that leave shadows behind her final work. She often smudges her papers when her hands are moist from perspiration. She cannot finish written assignments on schedule and is loaded down with unfinished work to be completed at home.

pieces fit together. They need to count fingers in math or touch their work as they figure things out. School work is time-consuming and exhausting for them. They cannot finish timed tests on schedule, which lowers their scores on standardized tests. They usually score several points below their actual level of intelligence on IQ tests. They rarely demonstrate the full extent of their knowledge or ability because they run out of time.

Time lag is a critical factor on standardized tests. It is easy to spot ADD patterns by looking at bar graphs of scores obtained from timed standardized achievement tests. Figures 1.9 through 1.12 show, for a single student over a 4-year period, the types of scatter that usually indicate ADD. This scatter reflects the tendency to guess when time runs out. It also reflects cycles of mental burnout that let the student do well for a while, then fall apart before the task is completed. This type of score scatter also reflects random marking of answer spaces on answer sheets that are separate from the test question booklet. Students who have ADD almost never do well when they must mark answer spaces on a different sheet. Having to refocus back and forth from the test to the separate answer sheet greatly increases the risk of mental burnout and random guessing for these students.

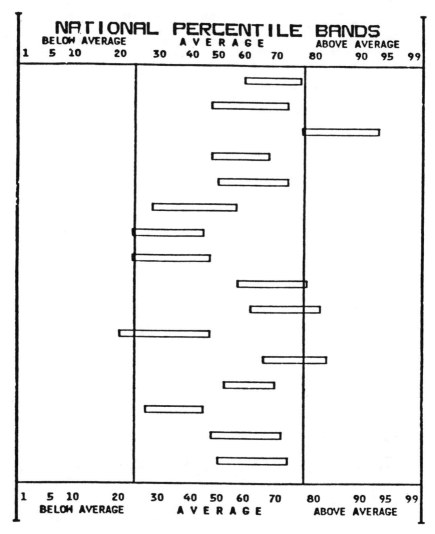

FIGURE 1.9. Scores of Jay, who has ADD, when he was in 7th grade.

Trouble Naming and Describing

Loose memory patterns make it impossible for students who have ADD or ADHD to recall precise terminology the moment it is needed. For example, names of geometric shapes continually mix together or disappear from memory completely, leaving the person with a shape that he or she misnames or cannot name on command. Names of math signs disappear, leaving the person to grope for what to say. Terminology in science

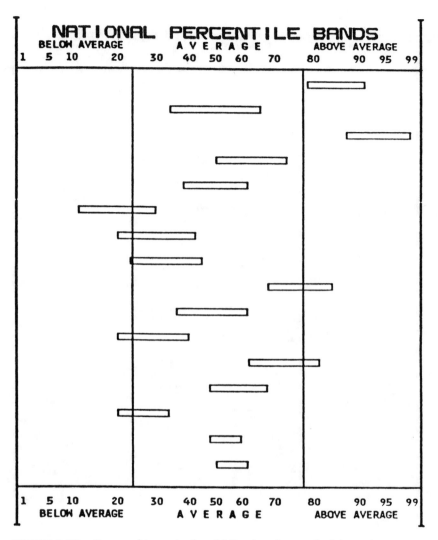

FIGURE 1.10. Scores of Jay, who has ADD, when he was in 8th grade.

and social studies evaporates from memory, leaving the student stuck with only half an answer. Such tasks as determining what to say, what to call things, or how to describe an event are frustrating and difficult for the person who has ADD or ADHD. Standardized test scores, especially on timed intelligence tests, are often much lower than the actual level of knowledge. On-the-spot demands for an answer often leave this student unable to respond; however, when the student has all the time he or she needs to search and ponder, adults are often surprised at the sophisticated knowledge actually possessed by the struggler who has attention deficit.

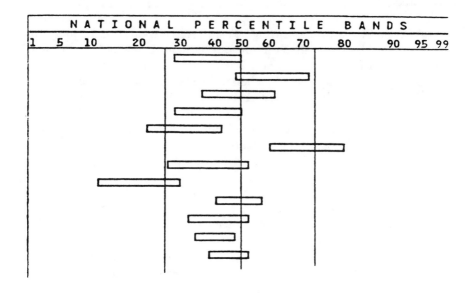

FIGURE 1.11. Scores of Jay, who has ADD, when he was in 9th grade.

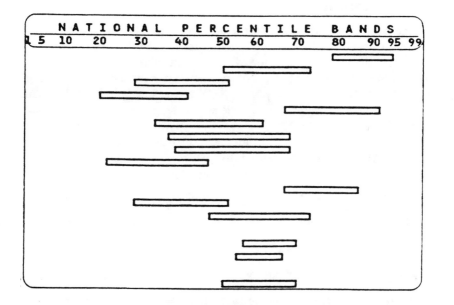

FIGURE 1.12. Scores of Jay, who has ADD, when he was in 10th grade.

Students who have ADHD or ADD tend to struggle with certain sub-tests of the *Wechsler Intelligence Scale for Children–Revised* (WISC-R) or the *Wechsler Adult Intelligence Scale–Revised* (WAIS-R). Scores on four sub-tests are usually lower than on others, producing a sawtooth pattern on the Wechsler score profile. These struggling learners usually show dips in Arithmetic, Coding (Digit Symbol), Information, and Digit Span. Diag-nosticians often look for this ACID pattern on Wechsler profiles. Figure 1.13 shows a typical ACID (sawtooth) score profile of a boy who has ADD. In the classroom, he does not have behavior problems. He is usually quiet and passive and seldom draws attention to himself. His struggle with aca-demic work is constant but low key. The chart in Figure 1.13 lets us see at a glance several important sets of information from his WISC-R per-formance. The left-side and right-side columns are the IQ scores that each Standard Score on the WISC-R yields. The rightmost column shows the percentile rank of each subscore. Across the top are the subtests from the WISC-R. The line graph vividly shows the extreme difference between the student's highest area of intelligence (Picture Completion with Stan-dard Score 15 and IQ 135) and his lowest areas of performance. Notice the 67-point spread between this boy's highest and lowest IQ scores on the WISC-R. Most students who have ADD or ADHD display this kind of extreme score difference and sawtooth scatter on the WISC-R and WAIS-R.

Oral Footnoting

Listeners who have ADD often make oral footnotes as they follow a stream of oral information. To anchor specific details of what they hear, they respond with vocal sounds, short words, or partial repeating of what they are hearing. In listening to a set of instructions, a listener who has ADD might say, "OK . . . um . . . yeah . . . OK . . . yes . . . um . . . OK." This goes on while the speaker talks. Or the oral message might be paraphrased, "Turn the knob . . . on 12 . . . close it . . . five times." This provides a quick repeat digest of what has just been heard. Sometimes the listener who has ADD turns statements into questions:

Speaker: Open your book to page 97.

ADD Listener: Ninety-seven?

Speaker: Now, start with the first paragraph.

ADD Listener: First paragraph?

Speaker: Now copy the first line.

ADD Listener: Copy it?

Wechsler Intelligence Scale Score Equivalents

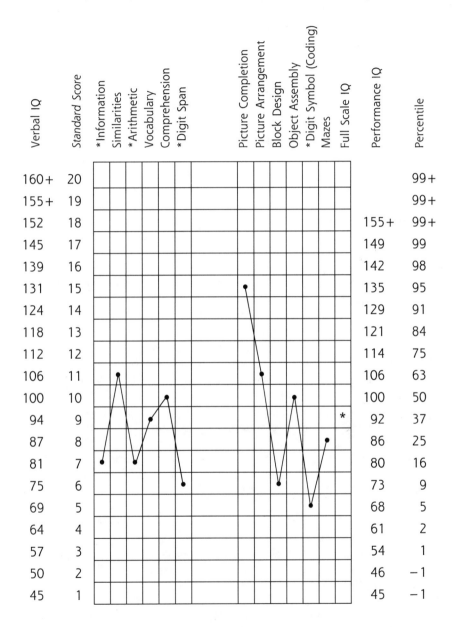

FIGURE 1.13. Typical ACID (sawtooth) pattern of a student with ADHD or ADD. This boy is 12 years, 8 months old in Grade 6.3. He struggles in all areas of formal academic work.

For many students who have ADD, this oral feedback (making oral footnotes) is an essential part of understanding what they hear. It is impossible for these students to develop full mental images of oral information without making a vocal response. This is actually a form of multisensory compensation. By hearing it and saying it, they combine two sensory pathways simultaneously. This is often enough to create a firm mental image that they can hold long enough to use what they have just heard. If oral footnoting is forbidden, these students are helpless to interpret and retain what they have received through listening.

ADD Syndrome, Residual Type

The 1980 DSM-III included an important category, ADD syndrome, residual type (DSM-III, 314.80), which referred to persons who carried their childhood attention deficit patterns into their adult lives. As they passed through puberty into adulthood, they did not outgrow the ADHD or ADD patterns described earlier in this chapter. The 1987 revision (DSM-III-R) eliminated the residual-type designation. Nevertheless, our culture feels the impact of immature, dyslogical adults who cannot establish stable lives because they still behave like the ADHD or ADD youngsters they used to be. This lifelong dilemma was well documented by Weis and Hechtman (1986) in their study of hyperactive children grown up.

Approximately 80% of those who have ADD as children begin to outgrow their symptoms during puberty (Hagerman, 1983; Jordan, 1988, 1989). Fewer than half of the children with ADHD outgrow their hyperactivity as they pass through adolescence (Taylor, 1990; Wender, 1987). Onset of puberty usually brings brain chemistry into better balance. Hormone production during puberty usually increases the maturity of the myelin structure, which is essential for good thought processing within the brain.

It is important to visualize attention deficit patterns along an index line that shows varying levels of severity:

0	1 2 3	4 5 6 7	8 9 10
none	mild	moderate	severe

For approximately 80% of children who have ADD, the level of severity declines as puberty advances. For example, at age 7½, a passive, daydreaming child who has ADD might be at Level 9 (middle of the severe range). This child cannot stay on task without supervision, cannot do assignments without constant monitoring, and cannot do chores independently. This child behaves much like a loose, late-maturing youngster of age 5½. As physical maturity begins about age 11 or 12, he or she might move down the severity scale to Level 8 (low side of the severe range).

By age 14, after 2 years of hormone activity within the central nervous system, this child might be down to Level 7 (high side of the moderate range). Although this student still needs a lot of supervision, guidance, and help, he or she is definitely becoming less dependent. By age 16, this student has moved down to Level 6 on the severity scale, with noticeable improvement in all areas of memory, responsibility, and success. By age 18, this person is functioning at Level 5 (middle of the moderate range). By age 21, this adult with residual ADD is down to Level 4. Still further growth (less struggle) will be seen about age 25, as this person reaches Level 3 on the severity scale. For most students who have ADD, physical maturation steadily improves the ability of the central nervous system to succeed with school learning and social development. This steady improvement continues into the mid-20s 80% of the time.

As Weis and Hechtman (1986) described, a person experiences a slow, steady decline in the severity of ADHD as he or she passes through puberty and reaches his or her mid-20s. However, the decline of hyperactivity is less pronounced than the progress of those who have ADD. Approximately half of children who have ADHD do not outgrow their primary symptoms as they enter adulthood, although improvement is usually evident. A child with ADHD who is at Level 9 at age 7 will likely be down to Level 7 by age 18. He or she will likely be down to Level 6 by age 23. At least half of those who have ADHD patterns as children will continue to have enough ADHD behaviors as adults to make life difficult and frustrating for them and their life partners.

The following sections describe typical characteristics of adults with residual-type ADD syndrome.

Poor Organization

The adult who has residual ADHD or ADD may or may not still be hyperactive. A majority of children exhibiting hyperactivity outgrow most of that pattern, regardless of whether they outgrow other attention deficit characteristics. One of the most striking earmarks of residual-type ADD is poor organization in adults. These men and women are poorly organized in most ways. They are habitually late to appointments and meetings. Job tools or materials tend to be scattered all over the place. Important things are continually lost or misplaced. These adults usually leave a trail of things behind with constant cluttering of workspace. Schedules are not followed. Deadlines are not met. Bills are not paid on time. Plans are not followed through. Housekeeping is haphazard. The person's car tends to be filled with "trash" that is seldom emptied. This adult's space is like that of the child with ADHD or ADD because the brain does not maintain an organized impression of time, space, or things within a given space.

Poor Listening

The adult who has ADHD or ADD is a poor listener. Important oral information is continually misperceived or misunderstood. Oral messages are remembered in a cluttered or scrambled way, leaving different impressions than were intended by the speaker. This adult does not develop a cumulative mental image as new oral information is received through listening. This person cannot repeat what was just heard without leaving out important chunks or scrambling the order of the information. He or she usually takes poor notes at lectures or discussions. The preservation of oral information through notes tends to be incomplete and inadequate. Adults who have ADHD or ADD are at a distinct disadvantage in listening situations. Telephone messages are misunderstood, conversations are remembered incorrectly, and radio or television news is misinterpreted. Lectures and sermons are only partly comprehended. Oral instructions are inadvertently changed so that the listener who has ADHD or ADD performs the task differently from how he or she was told. Names of people are misunderstood, and new names of places or things are lost. This adult struggles in any task that requires good listening.

Emotional Sensitivity

Adults who have ADHD or ADD tend to be overly sensitive. It is not unusual to find a truly paranoid frame of mind in which the person's first impulse is to jump to self-defense instead of hearing what is actually being said. This person has suffered criticism all of his or her life. Childhood ADD or ADHD patterns kept this person in continual conflict with adult expectations. As the sensitive years of teenage development occurred, the criticism continued. Adults who have ADHD or ADD have never known praise that was not mixed with criticism. These individuals do not have the "emotional toughness" most adults develop during the process of growing up. Constructive criticism tends to trigger emotional outbursts, angry self-defense, and blaming others. Adults who have residual-type ADD or ADHD often are too touchy to have satisfactory relationships with others.

I receive many letters from adults who have identified themselves after reading about attention deficits. In January 1991, I received the following letter from an adult after she read the first edition of this book:

> I am a 27-year-old housewife with two children. I have just finished reading your book *Attention Deficit Disorder*. It has enlightened me very much. I did not read this because my kids have this problem, instead I now know I myself do and always have.
>
> All through my school years I was told by my parents and teachers that I didn't try hard enough or concentrate enough on my studies. When in fact

I had a very hard time retaining information, comprehending, and remembering what I had just learned. Also it was difficult concentrating on any one subject. Because of all this I just thought I was dumb and would never be a very intelligent person.

I tend to be more the passive ADD syndrome type, who is overly sensitive and on the defensive a lot of the time. I read that 20% of the people with this problem do not outgrow it, this must be me, and I would like to know what I could do to overcome or live with this problem.

Short Attention

Becoming adult does not lengthen the attention span of people with residual-type ADD or ADHD. Attention to a given task remains short, with the tendency to drift off on mental rabbit trails. The adult with ADD or ADHD has great difficulty with conversation. This person may ask an intelligent question, then dart or drift to another topic before the speaker has uttered half a dozen words. It is highly disconcerting and irritating to try to converse with an adult who has residual-type ADD or ADHD. His or her thought patterns are loose and poorly organized, and the attention does not stay fixed longer than a few seconds at a time.

This adult is restless in audience situations. No matter whether the person is attending a concert, lecture, sermon, or demonstration, the attention darts or drifts away. He or she begins rustling the program or digging noisily into a purse or popcorn bag. There is a lot of sighing, coughing, and throat clearing, which irritates those sitting nearby. This adult shifts around in the seat, causing squeaks and visually blocking whomever is sitting behind. Every few minutes, he or she bursts into speech, whispering irrelevant things to a neighbor or asking an irrelevant question that distracts those nearby. It is virtually impossible for an adult who has ADD or ADHD to develop deeper appreciation of theater, symphony, opera, or other kinds of activities that require long concentration. This person is blocked from these kinds of satisfying interests because the thought patterns are too loose and short lived.

Difficulty Telling and Describing

The adult who has residual-type ADD or ADHD often has difficulty organizing his or her mental material to tell about an event or describe what happened. Speech is a series of bits and pieces that do not always emerge in the right sequence. Names are lost, the next word comes too slowly, and specific terminology is cluttered. If this adult tries to talk rapidly, the result sounds much like a speech defect with poor articulation. Sentences are chopped and scrambled, and the point of the story darts here and there. The oral flow reflects the loose, disorganized mental image that the adult who has ADD or ADHD is trying to verbalize.

Essential ingredients tend to be left out of the message. Later, this adult is frustrated, even angry, if the listener disagrees or seems not to understand. Emotional oversensitivity is often triggered when the adult who has ADD or ADHD thinks that the full message was delivered, but the listener realizes that something essential was scrambled or left out.

Short Job Tenure

Not all adults who have short job tenure have attention deficit disorder, but many do. It is often impossible for these adults to fit into typical job situations. Incomplete listening comprehension, trouble expressing ideas orally, overly sensitive emotional reaction to criticism, inability to follow a schedule, poor punctuality, and being too impulsive cause many adults who have residual-type ADD or ADHD to be poor job performers. The tendency is for this person to move from job to job frequently, seldom staying with any position longer than a few months.

Social Misfit

Adults who have ADD or ADHD are seldom able to fit successfully into typical social situations. The cluster of problems involving poor listening, misunderstanding, emotional sensitivity, poor oral expression, short attention, and poor organization keeps these persons from plugging into the flow of conversation. A majority of adults who have ADD or ADHD have very immature social skills. They tend to be isolated within the adult world, unable to blend into the interchange that is necessary for social success. Marriage relationships are difficult unless the spouse is a patient, easy-going person who allows plenty of time and is not bothered by poor organization.

Shoestring Baby Syndrome

For 17 years in private practice, I tracked patterns of attention deficit that seem to be related to distinct factors found in newborn infants (Jordan, 1988, 1989). This has been dubbed the shoestring baby syndrome, for want of a better label. Neither the 1980 DSM-III nor the 1987 DSM-III-R described this form of attention deficit disorder. The following sections describe patterns often seen in youngsters who have ADHD, as well as many of those who are passive yet have major problems with attention control.

Low Birth Weight

The term *shoestring baby* does not refer to premature infants of low birth weight, although such children often manifest attention deficit struggle.

The shoestring baby is a full-term infant, arriving within 2 or 3 weeks of scheduled delivery. Birth weight is low compared with birth length. Risk increases when birth length is 19 inches or longer, but birth weight is below 7 pounds. Examples of significant ratios that signal high risks for attention deficit disorder are as follows:

19 inches	5 pounds, 10 ounces
20 inches	6 pounds, 2 ounces
21 inches	6 pounds, 6 ounces

The probability of the child's having ADD or ADHD increases as the ratio between birth length and birth weight increases. The longer and "skinnier" the baby, the more likely it is that the child will display prominent attention deficit characteristics later on.

Problems of Infancy

Shoestring babies tend to have underdeveloped body systems. For example, they tend to have colic because of lactose intolerance. The digestive system is not mature enough in early infancy to digest milk. After a few months, digestion smooths out as enzyme production becomes stable and colic disappears. Immunity systems are also immature. Shoestring babies have repeated colds, sore throats, ear infections, bronchial congestion, and often pneumonia. As with the digestive system, these respiratory-type problems diminish as the baby matures.

Problems of Childhood

Shoestring babies are usually late losing baby teeth. Youngsters who have ADD or ADHD usually do not lose the first baby teeth until age 7 or 8. Children with normal physical maturity should lose lower front baby teeth by age 6½ and upper front baby teeth by age 7. Shoestring babies tend to be as much as 2 years behind that developmental schedule. Top front permanent teeth usually signal that all of the body systems are ready to handle classroom learning requirements. Shoestring babies are as much as 2 years late reaching this important developmental milestone. There is a high correlation between the age at which the top front permanent teeth emerge and the ability of the child to settle into good classroom listening, do assignments without help, and remember from day to day what is learned.

Social Isolation

Shoestring babies also tend to be late in other important developmental ways. The milestone of puberty is usually behind schedule. A majority of shoestring babies do not begin puberty until age 13½ to 15. This late development is especially difficult for boys. It is often devastating for a late-maturing boy in eighth or ninth grade to have to take showers with peers who are fully developed physically. This delayed entry into puberty is often a cultural and emotional shock from which sensitive late bloomers never fully recover. When puberty is delayed, as it is for a majority of these low birth weight youngsters, the social skills of teen years are also delayed. It is not unusual for these late-blooming boys to reach their early 20s before voice has fully changed, facial hair is abundant, and full body growth has been completed. These late developers cannot participate in typical teenage social life, which sharply compounds the many other problems caused by attention deficit disorder.

Summary

These are the categories of attention deficit disorder. Those people who manifest these patterns are at very high risk of failure in today's culture. Self-confidence is usually low because of chronic failure and living on the edge of failure. Self-image is usually low, and self-esteem is often negative because there has been too little praise and success upon which to build a positive feeling of self. These individuals often have little hope. As they look ahead, the future does not hold much more promise than the past, unless the attention deficit patterns are recognized early enough for help to be extended. Persons with these attention deficits tend to be second-class citizens in our competitive society where great emphasis is placed upon rapid achievement and fast productivity. It is critical that these syndromes are recognized early enough to change the course of failure into success. As we shall see in Chapter 4, if ADHD or ADD patterns are correctly identified and appropriate help is administered before ego structure is too badly crushed by failure, improvement is possible for these individuals.

Checklist of Attention Deficit Disorder Patterns

Adults who must deal with ADHD or ADD behavior often need an outline of the patterns that trigger conflict or create difficulties in the home, at school, or on the job. This checklist allows parents, teachers, tutors, or employers to pinpoint patterns found most often in individuals who have attention deficit disorder.

Hyperactivity

_____ Excessive body activity.
_____ Cannot ignore what goes on nearby.

_____ Cannot say "no" to impulses.
_____ Cannot leave others alone.
_____ Cannot spend time alone without feeling nervous or left out.
_____ Cannot leave things alone.
_____ Cannot keep still or stay quiet.

Passive Behavior

_____ Below normal level of body activity.
_____ Reluctant to become involved with group activity.
_____ Tries not to be involved in group discussion.
_____ Avoids answering questions or giving oral responses.
_____ Does not volunteer information.
_____ Prefers to stay alone in play situations.
_____ Avoids being included in games.
_____ Spends long periods of time off in own private world.
_____ Uses fewest words possible when required to talk.

Short Attention

_____ Cannot keep thoughts concentrated longer than a short period of time.
_____ Continually off on rabbit trails.
_____ Must continually be called back to the task.
_____ Drifts or darts away from task before finishing.

Loose Thought Patterns

_____ Cannot maintain organized mental images.
_____ Continually loses important details.
_____ Cannot do a series of things without starting to make mistakes.
_____ Cannot remember a series of events, facts, or details.
_____ Must have continual help to tell what has happened.
_____ Cannot remember a series of instructions.
_____ Cannot remember assignments over a period of time.
_____ Cannot remember rules of games.
_____ Keeps forgetting names of people and things.

Poor Organization

_____ Cannot keep life organized without help.
_____ Continually loses things.
_____ Cannot stay on schedule without supervision.
_____ Cannot remember simple routines from day to day.
_____ Lives in a cluttered space.
_____ Cannot straighten up room or desk without help.
_____ Cannot do homework without supervision.

Change of First Impressions

_____ First impressions do not stay the same.
_____ Mental images immediately change.
_____ Continual erasing and changing as writing is done.
_____ Has impression that others are "playing tricks" because things seem to shift and change.
_____ Continually surprised or startled as things seem different.
_____ Word patterns, spelling patterns, math problems seem to change.

Poor Listening Comprehension

_____ Cannot get the full meaning of what others say.
_____ Continually says "What?" or "What do you mean?" as speaker finishes oral message.
_____ Interrupts speaker by clamoring "What?" or "Huh?" or "What do you mean?"
_____ Cannot follow oral instructions without hearing again.
_____ Needs to have oral information repeated and explained again.
_____ Does not keep on listening.
_____ Drifts or darts away before speaker has finished talking.
_____ Later insists "You didn't say that" or "I didn't hear you say that."
_____ Cannot remember later what speaker said.

Time Lag

_____ Long pauses before student reacts.
_____ Does not start assignment without being pushed or guided to start.
_____ Long periods of time go by with no work done. Long pauses while student searches memory.
_____ Much whispering to self as student searches memory for information.
_____ Continually falls behind the pace of group activity.
_____ Does not stay on schedule set by teacher or group.

Overly Sensitive

_____ Immediate defensive reaction to criticism or correction.
_____ Blames others.
_____ Spends a great deal of emotional energy defending self or blaming others.
_____ Flies into tantrum when criticized.
_____ Jumps the gun, does not wait to receive all of the information before becoming angry or defensive.
_____ Leaders must spend a lot of time restoring calm and soothing hurt feelings.

_____ Defensive behavior forces leaders to spend a lot of time restoring calm and soothing hurt feelings.

Unfinished Tasks

_____ Does not finish any task without supervision.
_____ Leaves several unfinished tasks scattered around.
_____ Thinks task is finished when it is not.
_____ Does not realize when more is yet to be done to finish task.

Trouble Fitting in Socially

_____ Cannot fit into group situations without conflict.
_____ Whines or clamors for own way.
_____ Fusses about rules not being fair.
_____ Storms out of game when not winning.
_____ Wants to quit and do something else before others are finished.
_____ Is aggressive and domineering in order to get own way.
_____ Cannot carry on small talk as part of social events.
_____ Wanders about, avoiding personal involvement in social gatherings.
_____ Is insensitive to normal manners and protocol.
_____ Tends to be abrupt, rude, impolite in expressing opinions.
_____ Is overly critical of how social events are managed.
_____ Keeps conflict going over unimportant issues.
_____ Displays self-centered attitude instead of noticing needs of others.

Easily Distracted

_____ Attention continually darts to whatever is going on nearby.
_____ Cannot ignore nearby events.
_____ Continually stops work to see what others are doing.
_____ Overly aware of nearby sound, odor, movement.
_____ Cannot ignore own body sensations.
_____ Must scratch every itch, adjust clothing, touch or feel objects.

Immaturity

_____ Behavior obviously less mature than expected for that age.
_____ Behaves like much younger person.
_____ Cannot get along well with agemates.
_____ Prefers to play or be with younger persons.
_____ Has interests and thought patterns of much younger persons.
_____ Does not make effort to "grow up."
_____ Refuses to accept responsibility or be responsible.
_____ Behavior is impulsive/compulsive.
_____ Acts on spur of the moment instead of thinking things through.
_____ Refuses long-range goals.

_____ Insists on immediate satisfaction of wishes and desires.
_____ Puts self ahead of others.
_____ Blames others for own mistakes.
_____ Triggers displeasure of companions.
_____ Is often disliked by others.

Insatiability

_____ Desires are never satisfied.
_____ Clamors for more.
_____ Cannot leave others alone.
_____ Demands attention.
_____ Quickly bored and wants something different.
_____ Complains that others get larger share.
_____ Blames parents and leaders for not being fair.
_____ Drains emotions of those who must be involved with this person's life.
_____ Triggers desire in others to push this person away.
_____ Often dreaded by others.
_____ Becomes target of rejection by others.

Impulsivity

_____ Does not plan ahead.
_____ Acts on spur of moment.
_____ Does whatever comes to mind.
_____ Shows no common sense in making decisions.
_____ Does not think of consequences.
_____ Demands immediate satisfaction of wishes and desires.
_____ Is a "now" person.
_____ Cannot put off desires or wishes.

Disruptiveness

_____ Is disruptive influence in group.
_____ Keeps things stirred up.
_____ Triggers conflict within group.
_____ Disturbs neighbors during study time.
_____ Causes others to complain about how this person is behaving.
_____ Others are relieved when this person is absent.

Body Energy Overflow

_____ Some part of the body in continual motion.
_____ Cannot sit still.
_____ Cannot be quiet.

_____ Can hold body motions under control briefly, but overflow starts again soon.

_____ Fingers fiddle with things.

_____ Feet scrub floor.

_____ Legs bump desk.

_____ Body shifts around.

_____ Mouth makes noises.

Emotional Overflow

_____ Emotions always near the surface.

_____ Cries too easily.

_____ Laughs too loudly.

_____ Squeals too much.

_____ Giggles too often.

_____ Protests too frequently.

_____ Clamors in an emotional way.

_____ Easily triggered into hysterical state.

_____ Tantrums always near the surface.

Lack of Continuity

_____ Life does not have continuity.

_____ Lives life in unconnected segments.

_____ This event does not flow into next.

_____ Must have supervision and guidance to stay with a course of action.

_____ Present activity not connected in this person's mind with what happened previously or what will follow.

_____ Daily patterns and routines do not register.

_____ This person continually surprised by each task requirement, no matter how many times routine has been done.

Poor Telling and Describing

_____ Stumbles over words, names, and specific details while telling.

_____ Speech jumps around without following an organized theme.

_____ Speech made up of fragments instead of whole statements.

2

HOW ATTENTION DEFICIT DISORDER DISRUPTS ONE'S LIFE

The most accurate description of people having ADHD or ADD is to say that their life is constantly disrupted. Chapter 1 presented the many ways in which attention deficit disorder makes life difficult, frustrating, and unproductive. Ironically, parents, teachers, and even diagnostic specialists do not always recognize ADHD or ADD. The disruptive behaviors are often thought to be merely stubbornness, defiance, laziness, or lack of trying. In this chapter, we look at how attention deficit disorder disrupts one's life in the classroom, at home, and on the job.

ADHD and ADD in the Classroom

Regardless of which type of attention deficit a child might manifest, the basic problem in the classroom is inability to plug into the environment. Whether hyperactive or passive, this child does not absorb the environment in an effective way. New information presented in formal lessons does not enter the memory systems. New experiences within the group do not register as fully meaningful events. Important interactions that give meaning to relationships do not connect. The student with ADHD or ADD seldom comprehends more than 30% of what occurs around him or her (Jordan, 1988, 1989; Weis & Hechtman, 1986; Wender, 1987). New vocabulary is not added to the language stock on schedule. New data are not fully recorded by the mind. There is no steady, ongoing growth of skills in academic work or social development. In most ways, this child is a misfit in mainstream classrooms. The underlying inability to devote full attention to what occurs outside the self blocks the child's new learning. The student who has ADD or ADHD cannot fit into the regular world of education. These students bring a cluster of problems into the classroom, creating challenges that teachers cannot always meet.

Social–Behavioral Problems

Self-centeredness. Most youngsters who have ADD or ADHD are likable in one-to-one relationships. When they are alone with an adult or a playmate, a good relationship often occurs. These children are often deeply sensitive, feeling the same emotions felt by other intelligent youngsters. They care deeply for pets. They grieve over sorrow that comes into the lives of family and friends. They laugh and make jokes and have lots of fun when they are free to set their own pace in working out mental images.

Even though a child who has ADHD or ADD can be as delightful as any other person in a one-to-one situation, when he or she must enter a group and interact with several others for an extended period of time, a critical breakdown occurs. The person who has attention deficits spends most of the time dealing with his or her self. Inattention makes it impossible for these individuals to recognize the need to put self aside in the interest of others. However, these persons are not necessarily selfish. Many are generous to a fault in letting others have their things. The problem is that the personality structure is centered around the self. The individual who has ADHD or ADD is preoccupied by personal wishes, usually in the form of make-believe. These persons spend many hours off on private rabbit trails, mentally acting out stories or situations they invent, or being heroes in battles they imagine. Quiet ones spend long periods of time adrift in imaginary situations that would make quite remarkable movies. The body is often still, with no outward sign of activity, while the mind is busy developing a complicated fantasy scene. Children who have ADHD often act out their inner stories, physically rocking their chairs, turning furniture upside down for fortresses, and "marching" or "dancing" with feet drumming the floor. They begin to hum and mumble dialogues. They thrust imaginary swords, or do imaginary ballet swirls, or punch out an assailant in imaginary Kung Fu battles. Although the attention of the child is turned inward where he or she is the star of this private world, this overflow of imagination immediately disrupts the class, calling for disciplinary action from the teacher. Those individuals who eventually outgrow hyperactivity gradually stop this sort of self-centered fantasizing, but it is one of the more critical problems faced by teachers in the first several years of formal education. When the child is centered on self, there is little way that the student can be an effective member of a classroom group.

During this self-centered phase, the child who has ADD or ADHD spends most of the time on self-gratification: When do we go to lunch? How much more do we have to do? When can I go home? Did you see my new dress? I got a new ball from my uncle. I can't find my new pencil. I need to go to the restroom. I don't want to do any more work now. When can we go play? You know what I saw last night? These are the concerns of less mature youngsters who have attention deficits. These kinds of self-centered thoughts occupy most of their time. Formal learning in the classroom cannot penetrate this thicket of self-interest. It requires extraordinary effort on the teacher's part to break through this kind of self-preoccupation to implant new academic knowledge and skills. The self-centered student who has ADD or ADHD is often beyond the reach of others except in a one-to-one relationship where tight structure can be maintained by the adult.

Boredom.   When the student who has ADD or ADHD is pressed into group learning, a strong sense of isolation occurs. This student's central nervous system is not capable of plugging in the variety of events happening at the same time. Loose thought patterns cannot develop an organized sense of what the whole group is doing. Too many loose ends keep the child from following conversations or discussions well enough to be a responsive member. The student who has attention deficits cannot deal with a group environment effectively. In reality, this person is isolated from the streams of interaction taking place. Whether hyperactive or passive, this student is alone in the world of formal learning. Oral information given by the teacher to the group does not make sense. The purpose of workbook activities does not register. The student does not enter into the spirit of the group as skills are practiced. The individual who has ADD or ADHD cannot compete successfully, so he or she quickly becomes an outsider in any competitive task. Alone on this island in the stream of learning, this person has nothing meaningful to do. Copying from the board or working a page of math problems is risky and seems pointless. Caught in a group process that gives little pleasure and few rewards, this student rapidly becomes bored. Fingers go exploring for something to do. Attention wanders to something more interesting. Memory drifts to an experience that was lots of fun. Desire lingers over a wish that has not been fulfilled. Make-believe carries the mind away from the dull classroom into an exciting, rewarding fantasy adventure. Being bored is one of the most common classroom experiences for students who have ADD or ADHD.

Restlessness. Bored bodies soon become restless. With nothing meaningful to do, the student who has ADHD soon begins to seek something to do. One of the first signals of lost attention is restlessness, especially with hyperactive persons who have short attention. Restlessness creates distraction that intrudes on others. Wiggles cause the chair to shift or squeak. Shifting around in the seat causes noise and movement. Rustling papers or knocking books to the floor attracts attention. Aimlessly rolling the pencil back and forth on the table top or flipping edges of books with a fingernail sends distracting sounds to neighbors. Sighing, groaning, and explosive breathing add to disruptive body actions. Soon nearby classmates are distracted and begin to complain. Before long, the teacher reprimands the student. The student who has ADHD does not know why he or she is scolded all the time. "John, sit still!" he hears over and over. "Carl, stop making that noise!" he hears when he does not realize that he is making noise. Hyperactive students are continually standing up at inappropriate moments, leaving the desk to walk across the room, going too often to the pencil sharpener, lingering at the library table instead of returning to the desk, and staying too long in the restroom. These restless students cannot stay put. Overflowing body movement reflects the restless state of mind with which these persons live. Their minds "fidget" the ways their bodies do. This restless physical overflow is a major earmark of attention deficit disorder in the classroom.

Emotional Sensitivity. Like students with other forms of specific learning disability, persons who have ADD or ADHD live on the edge of failure. No classroom task is free from the hovering threat of failure. The quirks that continually block memory are like goblins dancing around the student's desk, threatening to cause mistakes at any moment. Students who live under this never-ending shadow of defeat are understandably sensitive. From their earliest days in formal education, they have been publicly criticized for "not trying harder." Teachers have said many times, "You didn't follow my instructions. Don't you ever listen when I explain?" Parents have said more times than they can count, "I've told you a dozen times. Don't you ever hear what I say?" Adults and peers have made comments and jokes about how forgetful the student is. "John would lose his head if it weren't fastened on" stopped being funny years ago to the youngster who has attention deficits. Being labeled "careless" or "lazy" is painful and embarrassing. Bearing that reputation as long as the person can remember is humiliating. Before the student who has ADD or ADHD has been in school very long, he or she has become quite emotional about these chronic accusations.

Students who have ADHD usually become outwardly defensive. They lash out at those who criticize them. They start fights to avenge their honor. They scheme ways to get even with adversaries who tease or make sarcastic remarks. Many playground and lunchroom scuffles are triggered by the fighting back of an overly sensitive person who has ADHD. Tragically, many overly sensitive adolescents become involved in antisocial behavior that brings them under the jurisdiction of juvenile authority. Their destructive behavior often began with classroom failure. After all, if a child does his or her best, but that best is never good enough, what is the child to do?

Quiet students who have ADD seldom storm out in overt self-defense. They tend to pull back into themselves, tuning out the classroom atmosphere that inflicts so much pain through failure. Their defense is often to become increasingly detached. If they do not hear what others say, they will not be hurt by the words. In defending themselves so passively, they also cut themselves off from classroom participation. Formal learning stops, but at least overly sensitive feelings are spared. It is possible for students who have ADD to build such thick, tough walls of passive self-protection that it becomes impossible for classroom teachers to reach through the barrier.

Misunderstanding.   The lives of most individuals who have ADD or ADHD are clouded by misunderstanding. These persons continually misunderstand what others say or mean, and others continually misunderstand their behavior. Well-organized adults who have no difficulty with their own thought patterns cannot believe that this student, who is healthy and bright, cannot do better. Teachers and parents tend to interpret attention deficit disorder patterns as disobedience, laziness, or lack of effort. Adults often try to force the disorganized student to function more effectively. However, no amount of discipline changes the patterns. If one adult gives too much supervision to get the child to function, another may say that too much coddling is going on: "John has to learn to accept responsibility on his own." If adults back away and place all responsibility upon the child, nothing improves. In fact, when students who have attention deficits are left alone to carry out responsibility, they are helpless.

Misunderstanding multiplies rapidly in the classroom. Instructions are misunderstood and not carried out by those who have ADD or ADHD. Comments made by peers are misinterpreted and blown out of proportion by these overly sensitive individuals. Peers misunderstand the halting speech of the classmate who has lost his or her words in trying to tell about something. Diagnosticians and other professionals who try to evaluate these struggling learners often misunderstand, not seeing the overall syndrome. It would be accurate to say that most persons who have ADD or ADHD are among the most seriously misunderstood individuals within our culture. They live most of their developmental years being mis-understood and failing to understand the world around them.

Insatiability.   As described in Chapter 1, the child who has ADHD is often insatiable. In the classroom, insatiable needs for personal attention and approval become an enormous problem. An insatiable student does not leave others alone. It is impossible for this person to study silently or alone. The need for feedback from others is overwhelming. The insati-able student clamors for the teacher's attention regardless of how much time the teacher has already spent in one-to-one contact with him or her. This person cannot stay in a designated space without someone to share that space. The insatiable person cannot leave classmates alone during independent study time. The insatiable student must have continual con-tact through touching, speaking, and being spoken to. This person is overly sensitive about being alone. When teachers and classmates become frus-trated and tell the insatiable one to leave them alone, his or her feelings are hurt. Sometimes there is an emotional outburst of self-defense as the rejected individual blames others for being selfish or not caring. Some-times he or she retreats into a pout, brooding about how unfair everyone always is. The insatiable person is extremely immature, unable to deal with the issues of life realistically.

The need for constant company overpowers every other need of the insatiable individual. He or she runs extreme risks to gain the attention of others. These students expose themselves to great risk of rejection or ridicule in order not to be isolated. An insatiable student is disruptive. This person places heavy pressure upon the emotions of the group. The insatiable person in the classroom demands much more than anyone can give. This person has no concept of privacy or appreciation of the terri-torial rights of others. The inner hunger for response from others over-whelms all other considerations as this individual clamors to be satisfied.

Impact of Failure on Self-Esteem.   The most devastating result of atten-tion deficit disorder is loss of self-esteem. As children progress through their developmental years, the normal pattern is to accumulate good stories to tell about personal success, prizes and awards received, and praise that was earned. Children who have ADHD or ADD are mostly left out of this normal developmental process. They do not win prizes for good work. Their papers are not displayed proudly on the bulletin board. Their report cards do not gain praise. In fact, most adult comments to a child who has attention deficits are negative in some important ways: John, you didn't follow my instructions again. Mary, you forgot to put your name on your paper again. Sam, this is the fourth time I have repeated my instructions. Don't you ever listen? Shelly, you forgot to give me your homework again. Robert, your handwriting must be neater. This litany of criticisms and complaints never ends for students who have ADD or ADHD. From the earliest years these students can remember, adults have been saying negative things about their behavior. There is no cumulative memory of praise and compliments and congratulations for jobs well done. Students who have attention deficits have few positive stories to tell. When they do tell stories, they often resort to make-believe to compensate for their history of failure. Then they are frequently accused of "lying."

Having no good stories to tell leaves deep scars upon a youngster's self-esteem. If everyone else has good stories to tell, but the child who has attention deficits does not, then the impression of self is negative and inferior. If everyone else succeeds in winning praise, but the child who has attention deficits hears only criticism and blame, the impression of self is that "I am not good." In later years, those who outgrow the academic problems of attention deficit disorder and become good students as adults continue to labor under the burden of low self-esteem. Being unable to satisfy adult expectations during the important developmental years of childhood implants deeply rooted impressions of the self as bad, inadequate, and of low value. The feeling of low self-worth is an unfortunate legacy when ADHD or ADD is not recognized early so that constructive help can be given.

Problems with Academic Learning

Poor Listening Comprehension.   Ability to understand a stream of oral information is very poor with students who have attention deficits. As a rule, the level of comprehension through listening is seldom higher than 30%. This means that the listener who has ADD or ADHD fully understands and retains only about one-third of what he or she hears in the course of a schoolday. This deficit in auditory perception has nothing to do with the ability to hear. These struggling students usually hear well enough; however, their central nervous systems do not connect meaning to the flow of words that come through listening. Sometimes these children interrupt by making oral footnotes, which was described in Chapter 1. Sometimes they respond with a puzzled "What?" or "Huh?" Sometimes they give no response at all as if they had heard nothing. When time lag is a factor, the student cannot develop a mental image rapidly enough to respond to what he or she just heard. Poor listening ability is a major obstacle in classroom performance for most students who have attention deficit disorder.

It is difficult for these individuals to participate in class discussions. The strands of oral information that are shared by several classmates during a discussion do not connect into a meaningful mental image for the listener who has ADHD or ADD. What John says does not connect with what Mary replies. The teacher's question has nothing to do with the answer recited by Paul. Again, the student who has attention deficits is on an island within a stream of flowing talk. The sense of isolation increases as others converse or discuss because it makes no sense to the poor listener. This isolation in listening intensifies the emergence of boredom and restlessness. The student who has ADD or ADHD is quickly lost in activities that require oral language to be processed and understood on another person's schedule.

Teachers face a continual problem in making new information clear to the listener who has ADD or ADHD. As the teacher explains a new procedure, gives oral instructions, or lectures on a specific topic, this student does not follow. Bits and pieces of the oral information may register, but this person does not develop a full mental image of what was said. This leaves him or her unable to put that oral information to use. As the teacher finishes giving instructions, she may ask, "Does everyone understand?" The student who has ADD or ADHD never does. The same student raises a hand every time, wanting to know what to do. The same voice is raised every time: "What are we supposed to do?" If the teacher points out that the student is not following instructions, he or she exclaims, "You never told me that," or "I didn't hear you say to do it." This scene is played again and again, hour after hour, day after day. The child's listening skills do not grow no matter how much scolding is done. The central nervous system of the listener who has attention deficit disorder is not capable of processing a flow of oral information and getting the full meaning of what was said to the group.

These poor listeners often do quite well in one-to-one relationships where the speaker watches for lost attention, then backs up and helps the person hear it again. One-to-one, the teacher can hold the student's thought patterns in tight enough focus to permit full understanding of what is heard. But in group activity where these strugglers are left to do their own structuring, their attention span is too short. Without being tightly guided, the listener who has ADD or ADHD drifts and loses the continuity of what he or she is hearing.

Unpredictable Response.   One of the most frustrating characteristics of attention deficit disorder is the tendency to do some early steps of a task well, then begin to make mistakes on later steps in the same task. This is frequently seen in math computation, as we saw in Chapter 1. Memory for math facts or how to carry or borrow is good for five or six problems at a time. Then the student who has attention deficits misses the next several problems partly or completely. On spelling tests, this student spells several words correctly, then misspells the next several words in a "careless" way, as we saw in Chapter 1. The time frame for doing fully accurate math or accurate spelling is short.

This short circuit pattern is not caused by carelessness, however. As the student works through a series of tasks, specific memory becomes spotty and unpredictable. Mental images that are clear one moment become cluttered and confused the next moment. Students with these short circuit patterns seldom maintain fully clear mental images for more than several seconds at a time. These youngsters are at a constant disadvantage doing assignments. No matter how hard they pledge to do better, their memory patterns trip them up. Promising to be more careful does not change this underlying neurological deficit.

This unpredictability in memory work is also seen in oral responses that students are asked to make. Ability to give specific answers from memory is spotty and unpredictable. These students continually lose their words. For example, no matter how many times they may have named geometric shapes or math signs, they stumble when naming a triangle, a rectangle, a square, a plus sign, or a minus sign. When these short circuits occur, the student is forced to stop, wait, search for the lost word, then try to give the answer the teacher is waiting for. If time is limited, as in most intelligence and achievement tests, these students cannot earn credit when the memory search takes too long.

Students who have ADD or ADHD suffer much embarrassment at school when adults make an issue of their trouble giving answers. If the child is scolded for not answering well, he or she is once more humiliated by the unpredictable ability to respond. These frequent cycles of being unable to answer accurately implant deep feelings of helplessness. This kind of invisible struggle with the names of things or with unexpected errors while working a string of problems does great damage to the sensitive self-image. It is impossible for students who have these memory deficits to develop positive self-image because they never know what will emerge when a specific response is called for.

Poor Organization. Lack of mental organization is a major source of friction in the classroom. The tools of learning are not seen by the student who has ADD or ADHD as an organized, integrated whole. A book lying on the floor does not seem out of place. A pencil left on the library table is not connected with the writing task that was interrupted when the student went to sharpen the pencil. As these loose, poorly organized students move through the day, there is no cumulative mental image of where things are or where they ought to be.

In a homeroom class where students stay all day, essential things are continually misplaced. When it is time for math, the math book is missing. When it is time for reading, yesterday's homework cannot be found. When it is time to draw, the crayons are not in the desk. Students in a departmentalized curriculum that requires the class to move to a different room each hour are at a serious disadvantage. If students who have ADHD or ADD must go to their lockers for new supplies several times a day, it is impossible for them to be on time to the next class. These students are forever tardy. If they must catch the bus immediately after school, they cannot remember what books to take home to do evening assignments. Parents who pick up children after school continually face the problem of something important being left behind. No amount of scolding or lecturing makes any difference. The central nervous system of these strugglers cannot maintain an organized, long range image of duties and responsibilities unless a written list is made for each set of expectations. Even then, the child who has attention deficits tends to lose the list. Poor organization is an earmark of this neurological deficit.

Distractibility.   When one is a member of a class group, progress depends upon being able to concentrate on the main activity while tuning out events that are not related to the central task. Children with normal neurological processing ability soon learn to ignore anything that is not important at each moment. Youngsters who have attention deficits cannot tune out the irrelevant successfully. Little events, such as nearby sounds, unexpected activity across the room, some movement out of the corner of the eye, or a sudden new odor, clamor for this child's attention. He or she darts off on that rabbit trail instead of saying "no" to the impulse. Eye control is lost at that moment, so the student loses the place in reading. Thought patterns are interrupted, so the student forgets what he or she was doing. Mental image of the task dissolves, leaving the student lost and wondering what to do after the distraction has been investigated.

It is impossible for these chronically distracted youngsters to finish a task. They continually leave jobs unfinished or assignments only partly done. They do not get all the way through a work page before attention is diverted. Then they do not manage to come back to finish the page. They tend to skip portions of the assignment, thinking that every step has been completed. Later, when adults scan the unfinished work, conflict is triggered as the student is accused of being careless or not paying attention to the work. Students who have ADD or ADHD leave holes in their work, as discussed in Chapter 1, not realizing that everything has not been done. Their memory recalls that work was being done, and when it stopped, it must have been because it was finished. These students are not aware that their attention was distracted. The small amount of work done seems to them to be the whole task.

Burnout.   As we saw in Chapter 1, most students who have attention deficit disorder have specific, measurable points at which a type of burnout occurs. For example, it is not unusual to find a time cycle of 90 seconds, 3 minutes, 5 minutes, or 7 minutes during which the student's full concentration on a task can be maintained. At the end of that time cycle, the student suddenly "loses everything." Often it is described as "going blank."

Jim Reisinger, a financial consultant in Ann Arbor, Michigan, realized his lifelong problem with ADD after reading the first edition of this book. In a letter to me, he described his ADD burnout as "blinks." He explained, "A blink is a period of time when the ADDer's attention invol-

untarily skips to a tangent thought. The effect is a lapse in the information flow.'' Reisinger told what it is like to live with this unpredictable
blink pattern. Without warning, his thoughts suddenly jump to a different topic. His mind is never blank, as many persons with ADHD or ADD
report. Something is always in his thoughts. For example, as he works
with a client, Jim finds himself off on a mental rabbit trail that may have
been triggered by a word or phrase he saw in the contract or heard the
client say. These moments at which his mental images blink are tied to
burnout. Once Reisinger reaches a certain point of mental fatigue, his tendency to blink and skip to a different thought increases dramatically.

For the person who has ADD or ADHD, burnout refers to the sudden
loss of ability to think, to analyze, or to continue doing that task. Quality
of work may have been quite good with few errors until burnout occurs;
then suddenly everything is wrong and a radical change occurs in the quality of work. Good spelling falls apart. Smooth left-to-right sequencing
begins to scramble. Accurate math computation becomes filled with errors.
Memory for the procedure is gone, leaving the student fumbling and grop-
ing for what to do next. Sentence structure falls apart, with fragments
appearing instead of full sentence form. Typing errors suddenly multiply
in the middle of smooth keyboard writing. Essay writing falls apart after
getting off to a good start. Students with these burnout points are bewildered, not understanding what is happening. Teachers are puzzled, not
understanding how this radical change can occur so frequently. Adults
who watch these daily burnout patterns often realize that the student is
doing his or her best, yet the effort deteriorates after a certain length of
time. Neurological burnout is one of the common problems of individuals with attention deficit disorders in the classroom.

Messy Papers. Most students who have ADHD have trouble writing
neatly and producing attractive written work. The central nervous system cannot maintain well-organized thought patterns during the act of
writing. Figure 2.1 illustrates this problem. This 13-year-old boy could
not copy from the board accurately. He was not dyslexic, which also causes
sloppy writing and mistakes in copying. Figure 2.1 shows the frequent
short circuits that continually interrupted his mental image as he transferred visual information from the chalkboard to his paper. All of this boy's
schoolwork had this appearance. His spelling papers were filled with
erasures and scratch-overs as he searched for a better way to write the
word. Math papers were almost impossible to decipher because of so many
errors in encoding. Book reports and other kinds of essay material were
so sloppy his teachers wondered if he ever tried to be neat.

The written work of students who have attention deficits is continually criticized and condemned. If teachers follow the practice of display-
ing the best papers on the bulletin board, these students almost never share
the glory of public praise for good writing. Written work is usually so frus-

Test 1

Daniel Boone was a courageous and
vigorous man. Years ago he
entered the American wilderness
with visions of all who would
follow the trail he blazed.
Westward migration did begin to
move over his pathways through

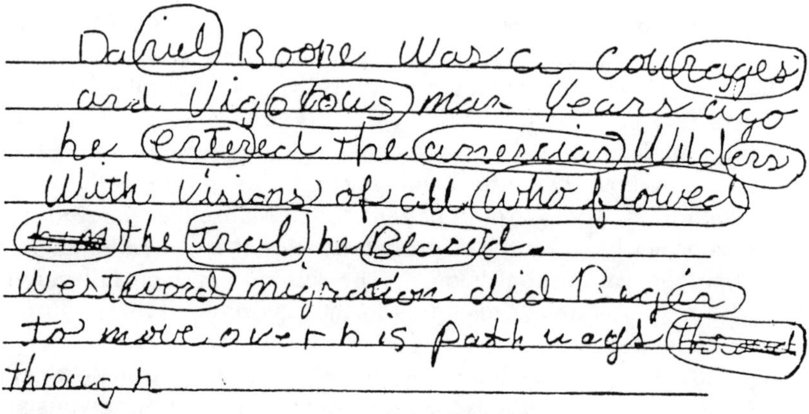

From Form D—Slingerland Screening Tests. Permission has been granted to reproduce this example.

FIGURE 2.1.   Written work of a boy aged 13 years, 1 month.

trating that these students develop a system for losing or hiding classroom papers. Teachers often find desks or lockers stuffed with assignments never handed in. The struggling student cannot take pride in his or her written work. It does not earn praise, and it often does not receive credit because of abundant errors and ''careless'' appearance. Fine motor coordination is often too unpredictable for these students to do better. Copying papers over or doing written assignments again does not improve the quality. It is often impossible for these struggling learners to produce neat, well-organized written work that is free from mistakes.

Erratic Reading Comprehension.   Most students who have attention deficits have adequate phonetic skills. Unless they are also dyslexic, they do not have disability with phonics. They tend to stumble over syllables within words, and they cannot always keep sound units in the right sequence, yet they usually know how to blend sounds together and how to chunk. According to diagnostic testing, phonics skills are often among the highest skills of these students.

However, reading comprehension tends to be low and unpredictable. The problem is similar to that found in listening to oral information. In listening to a stream of speech, the central nervous system of the student who has ADD or ADHD does not process everything that is heard. Only bits and pieces of what the person hears are comprehended and understood. The same problem occurs as the student reads. He or she may be able to sound out or correctly recognize every word on the page, but only bits and pieces of the meaning are recorded by the memory. The reader who has attention deficits does not develop a cumulative, ongoing mental image of what the text has said. He or she turns only some of the printed passage into inner speech. The author's written message does not become fluent inner language for the reader who has ADD or ADHD. He or she handles this inner language of reading in the same broken, choppy way the student listens. This reader leaves a reading task with only partial images of what was on the page. This makes it impossible for him or her to answer follow-up questions successfully.

The amount of material to be read is of critical importance for most students who have attention deficits. Short attention and rapid burnout sabotage the task of reading large quantities of text material. If teachers analyze the student's reading comprehension levels, wide fluctuations are evident from page to page. A typical attention deficit reading pattern might be 100% comprehension on the first page, 80% on the second page, and 40% on the third page. At that point, the student must stop because the reading task has become too frustrating. If he or she comes back after a brief rest, the level of comprehension usually climbs back to 80% or higher on the fourth page. Then it starts down again on the fifth page and reaches burnout again on the sixth page. Careful analysis shows that the reader had excellent comprehension part of the time but poor comprehension at other times within the same block of reading. Reading ability zigzags from high to low as time passes during the act of silent reading. It is impossible for these loose thinkers to benefit from sustained reading tasks. However, they can do good reading if the text is divided into short segments that fit the cycles of neurological burnout. This kind of planning can be plotted for readers who have attention deficits if adults pay attention to the burnout cycles that differ from student to student.

Avoidance of Work.   One of the most difficult problems teachers face in dealing with students who have attention deficits is keeping them at their work. Because of boredom, short attention, and drifting away from the task, these students face schoolwork with great dread. If they are overly sensitive about possibly being wrong, they often develop strong phobias when there is the chance they might make mistakes. Many students who have ADD or ADHD develop deeply ingrained habits of avoiding their work. They cannot tolerate the normal pressure of academic toil. They are too easily overwhelmed by the emotional surges involved with frequent failure. They spend a great deal of time and energy seeking ways to get out of doing assignments. These students often complain of "not feeling well." This can be based in very real discomfort—from eye strain, for example. If poor vision is part of the student's problem, then the reader usually does indeed have frequent headaches and not feel well. The person may fit the shoestring baby category that was described in Chapter 1. Immaturity of the digestive system or intestinal allergies to certain foods may cause gastric problems that keep his or her digestive tract in misery. However, most avoiders do not have actual physical problems. Pleas to "go to the restroom" or "go see the nurse" are usually efforts to avoid tasks that place too much stress on fragile skills.

Students who have ADHD avoid tasks any way they can. Pencil leads are broken every few minutes, requiring frequent trips to the pencil sharpener. It is easy to stretch a 45-second pencil sharpening chore into 2 or 3 minutes away from the desk. Or the student may want to look up a word in the unabridged dictionary that is across the room. This simple chore can be extended into a 15-minute search. Or the student may have left an essential item in the locker and ask for a hall pass. Once out of the room, it is easy to stretch a locker visit into 30 minutes. The fact that the student ends up in trouble for this kind of procrastination does not stop the avoidance patterns. To him or her, avoiding threatening work is worth the consequence.

Passive students who have attention deficits often develop another type of avoidance. Instead of overtly leaving the scene of the task, they silently drift away into daydreams. Sometimes they develop cover-up behavior of seeming to do the work while actually nothing is being accomplished. They learn how to look busy from across the room while spending the time adrift in a world of wishful make-believe. Later, they must face the consequences of work not finished, but their passive drifting helps them pass the time without becoming involved in doing the task. It is possible for these silent drifters to float for a year or longer before adults become aware that no skill development is taking place. If the student does just enough to avoid failing the class, he or she might float for several years, neither learning new material nor increasing important skills. The avoidance behavior of students who have ADD or ADHD is sometimes beyond the reach of the classroom teacher. If the tendency becomes too deep seated, there may be nothing effective the teacher can do to change the student's response to schoolwork.

These are the characteristics of attention deficit disorder in the classroom. The student's surface behavior appears lazy, disinterested, unmotivated, and careless. The student may drive everyone crazy by clamoring constantly, or he or she may simply drift in a silent way, intellectually apart from the mainstream learning taking place in the classroom. Scolding does not change the behavior. Forcing the student to work without help does no good. Poor organization, messy papers, and lost materials continue to frustrate both the teacher and the student day after day. Punishment does not bring better performance. Unless the underlying neurologically based problem is identified, years of conflict and a life of chronic failure are set into motion, with devastating effects upon self-esteem.

ADHD and ADD at Home

As we consider how ADHD and ADD disrupt the lives of parents, siblings, and other close relatives, we must keep in mind the severity scale we saw in Chapter 1:

0	1 2 3	4 5 6 7	8 9 10
none	mild	moderate	severe

The impact of ADHD or ADD upon the family depends upon the level of severity. An aggressive child with ADHD at Level 9 will create much more disruption than a passive child who has ADD at Level 5. The clearest way to see the impact of ADHD and ADD at home is to visit two families in which severe attention deficits exist.

James

I first met James when he was 8 years old. He is now 22 years old in his third year of college. James was born into a deeply religious family that worked hard to live according to Biblical teachings. Mr. and Mrs. Able proudly took their son to church when he was 3 weeks old. Partway through the worship service, they were called to the church nursery where their infant son was creating a crisis. His screams could be heard all over the church. At 3 weeks of age, he was fighting everyone who touched him or tried to hold him. Thus began years of disruption of the Able family's life as this newborn son brought his frustration and tantrums into their home. James fought his parents, sisters, and all of the relatives from the moment he came home from the hospital nursery. Nobody could reason with him. His demands were insatiable. His temper often turned violent and destructive. As he developed the ability to move about and handle things, the family lost the privacy they had found so important before his birth. Before he could stand alone or walk, James climbed like a squirrel. In no time, he could be at the top of the bookshelves in the family room. When he was 11 months old, his father caught the tall bookshelf as it began to topple on top of the baby. After anchoring it to the wall, Mr. Able packed away all of the pictures and crystal objects he and his wife had collected from vacation trips. By the time James was 12 months old, the house was stripped of anything breakable that he could possibly reach. Before his first birthday, his parents knew that the next several years of their lives would be difficult and hard to bear. They had no idea how they had produced this angry little tiger who demanded everything, gave nothing in return, and seemed bent on destroying the home life the Ables had worked so hard to establish.

As James grew older, he became the dreaded child of the neighborhood. He hurt several other children and was forbidden by their parents to play. He was so aggressive with pets that his parents were forced to give away their beloved cat and middle-aged dog. None of the grandparents or uncles and aunts could handle James's visits, the way most relatives enjoy having little ones in their homes. He was so hyperactive and aggressive that none of the older relatives could cope with his strength and disruptiveness. He lived on the very edge of danger with no fear or display of common sense. In fact, it appeared that he thrived on danger. James took fearful risks that no logical person would take. When he was 4 years old, he climbed to the top of the community water tower that was 200 feet tall. Four firemen finally brought him down after chasing him several times around the catwalk 180 feet above the ground. Like a squirrel, he climbed the tall tree beside the house and leaped to the roof, then down the drainpipe to the ground, over and over. It was impossible to take him shopping unless he was in a harness with a leash tied to his father's wrist. If he were not restrained, he would dash off into the shopping mall and disappear.

Mr. and Mrs. Able sought help from many sources. A child psychiatrist attempted psychotherapy with James and his parents. It was suggested that, as parents, the Ables were not doing their best with this child. If they paid more attention to him and less attention to themselves, surely their son would behave normally. The Ables went through several years of heavy guilt, believing that it was their failure that produced and kept alive their son's out-of-control behavior. They worked with two clinical psychologists who tried many kinds of management techniques. Nothing improved James's behavior beyond limited points. After making some improvement, he always went back to his aggressive, hostile ways. A series of pediatricians gave different opinions, none of which helped the Ables reduce the disruption in their home. Bedtime was a battle scene, with both parents physically forcing James to take a shower, brush his teeth, get into his jammies, and turn out the light. Evenings usually ended with his mother in tears, his father furious, and his sisters hiding in their rooms.

The only way bedtime was successful was for Mr. Able to shower with James, then lie down with the boy until he finally went to sleep. This procedure got everyone to bed, but it drove a wedge between husband and wife. James seemed to enjoy his power in keeping his parents apart at bedtime. Then next morning, he was up before sunrise racing about the house. He thrived on less than 6 hours of sleep. The rest of the family members were chronically exhausted.

James was dismissed from three preschools in town. By the time he was 4 years old, no preschool would accept him. Every child care agency in the community had heard of this uncontrollable little boy. When he was 5, his parents found a private kindergarten that reluctantly agreed to let James attend for 1 week to see if their staff could work with him. After 3 days, he was told not to come back. By this time, he had been labeled as emotionally disturbed, severely oppositional, and antisocial. By age 6, he was already beyond the reach of the educational systems of his community.

Meanwhile, the Able family was breaking apart. Mr. Able moved out of the house one night after he and his wife had a verbal battle. Both had become so frustrated over James's incorrigible behavior that each blamed the other for his condition. Words became increasingly bitter. Their anger had been building for several years without being properly channeled or expressed. When it all exploded, the marriage came apart. That night James climbed into his mother's bed and went right to sleep. With his father gone, he had his mother all to himself. His bedtime tantrums stopped and he began to act almost normally once he was in control. Mrs. Able confided to a close friend, "I am finding it very hard to love this child. When I look at my feelings honestly, I sometimes hate him. I am always angry at him. This makes me feel like a total failure as a mother. This child has cost us our marriage. We have not had a moment's peace since he was born. What am I going to do?"

The Ables were mature enough to patch things together so that the marriage survived, but the home was not a happy place. Finally, the grandparents put together enough money to enroll James in a special day school for emotionally disturbed children. Under the constant supervision of specialists in abnormal behavior, he learned to behave differently enough to remove some pressure from his home.

When he was 8 years old, James's parents brought him to me for an evaluation of his intelligence, learning patterns, and basic academic skills. I spent an entire day with this hyperactive boy who had been disruptive in every situation so far in his life. An amazing bonding occurred that day between James and me. Instead of forcing him to do the tests in traditional ways, I worked out ways for him to be himself as we did the activities together. Sometimes he lay on the floor with feet bumping the underside of the work table while I asked questions and he answered. At times he rolled back and forth on the large beanbag and chanted responses in little rhymes he created on the spot. Sometimes he sat in my lap and snuggled back against my chest. Then he lay flat on the carpet and pounded rhythms with his fists and feet. It was the first time in his life that he had been able to interact with an adult in such a comfortable way. There were no pressures, no threats, and no fears of failure. The novelty I allowed him to invent brought his thoughts together in multisensory ways. Fourteen years later, he still talks about that day when he met an adult who did not fight his hyperactivity but accepted him as the intelligent, creative person he really was.

James was at Level 10 on the severity scale when we met. His presence in his home exerted enormous pressure on everyone involved. He was totally disorganized and had no sense of how things should go or be arranged. He was insatiable, never receiving enough to satisfy him. He was completely self-focused, spending his energies on meeting his own desires and needs. He was angry, taking out his frustrations on anyone within reach. He was frightened and experienced awful nightmares that terrified him for days. He was phobic about many things that overloaded his sensory channels. For example, the sight of an inflated balloon sent him into hysterics. "It might pop!" he would wail, no matter where the family might be, and they would have to leave the restaurant or party or shopping mall where balloons were on display. James was often vindictive, going out of his way to get even with anyone who offended him or made him angry. He had no friends, no playmates, no pets, and no group of peers who would accept him. In all of this, he was bewildered. Why did the other kids not like him? Why could he not spend a week at Grandma's house? Why did his family stop going to Sunday School? Why did everyone always yell "No!" and "Stop that, James!"? When he and I met, he was a lonely, frightened, stubborn, uneducated boy with severely underdeveloped social skills. Yet he had enormous potential that lay beyond our reach. What could we do to help this severely handicapped child who showed many signs of ADHD?

Mr. and Mrs. Able were desperate for help with their son, yet they were afraid of medication that had been suggested by several pediatricians. (In Chapter 3, we will look at medications that often reduce ADHD symptoms in children such as James.) The Able family had heard too many "ghost stories" of children being made into zombies and growth being stunted by medication to control hyperactivity. Referring them to a physician for medication was out of the question. In our city lived a psychiatrist who was regarded by the professional community as being a "maverick." For several years, he had practiced what he called "ecological psychiatry." This method used diet control with hyperactive persons who did not respond to typical treatment for emotional disturbance or aggressive behavior. I asked the Able family whether they would be willing to let him try to help their son.

Because the treatment involved foods but no medications, James's parents agreed to try. The approach was direct and simple. James was the guest in a private clinic for a week. He was treated like a very important person, and he was introduced to computers that kept him busy. At the same time, he was systematically tested for food sensitivities. The Ables were asked not to see the boy or call him during the first 4 days. Because of our strong bond, I visited James and spent time watching him work with his computer. He went through strong withdrawal symptoms for the first 3 days as his body cried out for his old diet. He had monstrous tantrums and headaches. But he made it through that difficult time. An amazing difference was seen when I visited him on the fourth day. He was relaxed and quiet. He was laughing over some jokes he had printed on the computer. He snuggled into my lap with deep affection without any of his old games to control. That morning his attention span was the longest I had ever seen. We began working with phonetic skills he had never learned. The old disruptive James was out of the picture when his parents visited that day. They had never before seen their son able to interact in normal ways that were filled with affection.

James and his family began to follow a careful diet that was developed as his cytotoxic foods were identified. He was severely allergic to white wheat in any form. He could not tolerate milk. He had strong reactions to several foods in the salicylate group (green pepper, strawberries, tomatoes). He was highly sensitive to yeast, and he could not tolerate caffeine. When these culprit ingredients were taken out of his diet, he became relatively calm and reachable. On this new diet, James came down to Level 6 on the ADHD severity scale. He was still antsy and easily bored, except with computer activities. He still lost his temper and needed a lot of supervision. He still balked and could be very stubborn. He still had to be supervised because of poor organizational ability. However, as long as he avoided culprit foods and beverages, he was a comfortable member of his family. He learned to function in academic work and eventually became a good student. Now he is looking forward to graduate school where he will specialize in child psychology. His goal is to work with children who have attention deficit disorders.

The point of this story is that in his natural state, James placed so much stress upon his family it finally broke apart. Without intervention, which is discussed in Chapter 3, the home could not survive his uncontrolled ADHD patterns. The combination of hyperactivity and emotional battering was so disruptive neither the child nor his family could survive.

Nate

I met Nate almost by accident when he was 9 years old. After speaking to a parent group about attention deficit disorders, I was followed to my car by a woman who was crying. She had trouble talking through her sobs, but finally she was able to say, "You have just described my son. All these years I have tried to find out what his problem is. Tonight you have explained it. Everything you said about ADD without hyperactivity fits him to a tee.'' The more the mother talked about her son, the more I wanted to meet him. She was a single parent with two children. By working an extra part-time job on weekends, she was able to provide a modest living for her family. She told me how no one in her family wanted anything to do with her son. ''They call him weird,'' she explained. ''His dad has nothing to do with him, and none of the grandparents pay any attention to him. Can you help me with my son?''

Soon after that I met Nate. He is now 21 years old and in college, where he is specializing in computer science. But that first meeting was one of the strangest experiences of my life. Nate was unusually tall for his age. He was thin and awkward with poor motor coordination. I was greatly surprised to notice that he carried a Raggedy Andy doll. Nate introduced me to Roy, his doll. He placed Roy between us on the large round table where I worked with youngsters. He took a piece of gum from the candy dish and unwrapped it for Roy. He fussed with Roy's clothes and made all kinds of little sounds. He began speaking a singsong language I had not heard before. First Nate talked to Roy in the singsong voice. Then Roy ''answered'' in a high-pitched, whining response. This conversation between Nate and his doll lasted several minutes. Finally I realized that Nate was telling Roy why they were in my office. He was assuring Roy that everything was fine. As I learned how to interpret this private language, I heard Nate explain, ''Mommie thinks something is wrong with me and wants me to talk to this doctor. But nothing is wrong with me, is there, Roy? And nothing is wrong with you, either. This doctor just wants to ask me some questions, Roy. He is not going to hurt me or give me any shots or any medicine. He is going to tell Mommie that I am fine and that I don't need any shots or medicine. But it's OK, Roy. Don't be afraid. This nice doctor isn't going to hurt you. Now don't cry like that, Roy. Don't be afraid. It's OK, Roy.''

This litany continued for more than 10 minutes as I listened with fascination. Here was a 9-year-old boy, as tall as most adolescents, speaking a private language to his doll, making sure that the doll was not afraid. No wonder Nate's relatives called him weird. I knew from the mother's information that Roy did not go to school with Nate; however, the moment the boy arrived home from after-school care, he dashed into his room to be with Roy. They stayed behind the closed door until supper was ready. If Nate had his way, he would spend all of his time alone in his room talking things over with Roy in their private singsong speech.

As I worked with Nate over a period of time, we became close friends. However, it was more than a year before he came to me without bringing Roy. By working slowly and gently with Nate, I discovered that he had major ADD patterns. Beneath his quiet, withdrawn surface was a cluster of attention deficits that blocked him in many ways. I finally determined that he was at Level 7 on the ADD severity scale. No doubt he had been at Level 8 when he first started attending school. Listening comprehension was very poor. He understood less than 30% of what he heard unless someone repeated for him. His thought patterns were extremely loose. He rarely went longer than 90 seconds without losing his mental image. He continually experienced the "blink" patterns described earlier by Jim Reisinger. Without warning, the thought of the moment skipped to a different mental image. Along with this blink pattern were moments of going blank, when he lost his thoughts altogether. As I worked with Nate, I remembered a story told to me by a bright 8-year-old girl who had ADD. I asked her to tell me in her own words what it is like to have ADD. After thinking for a while, she said, "One time my family visited Silver Dollar City in Missouri. I saw an old telephone thing like they had when my Granny was a little girl. I saw this lady stick plugs in when someone called. Having ADD is like that, only my plugs keep falling out." And so did Nate's. No matter how hard he tried to keep on listening, thinking, or doing his work, his plugs kept falling out and he was lost.

On the surface, we might wonder how a passive, intensely private boy who spent most of his time doing make-believe with his doll could be disruptive within his family. However, the more I learned about Nate, the more easily I understood how disruptive his passive ADD patterns were for his mother, sister, and relatives. Nate had almost no sense of time passing, and he had no sense of organization. His room was a mess and he never attempted to clean it up. The small house in which the family lived was littered by things he inadvertently left lying around. His clothing was scattered everywhere. He was extremely slow starting to do a task, then very slow doing it. He never went from start to finish without being supervised. He could not remember to get home with necessary school materials. After supper, when his mother asked if he had any homework to do, Nate usually could not remember. On those days when he did get home with his stuff, he invariably forgot to take finished assignments and books back to school the next day. Every morning involved his mother nagging him, Nate dawdling and procrastinating, and mother and son having a shouting match because time was running out. Visits to relatives were equally frustrating and discouraging for Nate's mother. He refused to go without Roy his doll. This ritual behavior drove his mother wild. In spite of the snickers and teasing Nate received from relatives, he would not go without his make-believe partner. He sat in his grandmother's living room talking to Roy in their private singsong language even when adults showed their irritation. Then Nate would overhear some adult criticism that hurt his feelings. His mother could not remember a visit that did not end with Nate crying, relatives criticizing her for not making him throw away that doll and grow up, and her yelling at Nate all the way home. The boy's immaturity, fears, ritualized behaviors, and deep-seated fantasies expressed through his doll were highly disruptive to this single-parent household where the mother exhausted herself to earn a living and had to come home each night to this "weird" child.

Summary

Children who have ADHD or ADD above Level 5 on the severity scale are indeed disruptive at home. As discussed in Chapter 1, these youngsters press their environments hard. Their needs are never fully met. Their behavior is irregular and often embarrassing. Their invisible phobias and hidden agendas keep others on edge because these children cannot put their fears into words or turn them loose. Lack of organization causes their space to stay cluttered and untidy. Poor sense of time passing causes them to march to a different drum beat, always out of step with schedules that busy families must keep in order to survive. Arguments continually spring up over issues that seem picky and unimportant until we recognize how frustrated parents and siblings have become. These children who have attention deficits either race too fast and create messes from hurrying, or they dawdle along, creating anger and frustration because they do not hurry. They forget deadlines, lose their things, make excuses, hide behind fantasy that is often labeled as "lying," and demand attention for themselves with no concern for the welfare of others. They often develop rituals and refuse to give them up.

Home life with a child who has ADHD or ADD is invariably less than satisfactory. In severe cases, like that of James, marriages fall apart and grandparents pull back because they do not have the strength to cope with the situation. In single-parent families, as well as in two-parent households with limited income, there often is not enough money to afford the extra help required by the child with attention deficits. Parents of these children often are forced to spend limited funds on the child who has ADHD or ADD at the expense of other children who can get by without special help. The level of exhaustion is very high in these homes. Lack of privacy for parents and siblings becomes acute. It is not unusual to hear parents and siblings of the child with severe ADHD speak of abuse. Parents and siblings do indeed feel abused when children like James go several years unchecked. Attention deficit disorder, whether hyperactive or passive, brings high levels of stress and disruption into most homes where it exists. In Chapter 3, we shall find ways to help. There are ways to reduce disruptiveness if parents are willing to follow certain steps.

ADHD and ADD on the Job

Since the 1970s, there have been dramatic changes in the workplace. A generation ago, virtually anyone could find at least part-time work flipping hamburgers, pumping gas at a filling station, loading freight in a warehouse, or taking care of small children. Few of us foresaw how these simple jobs would change. By the end of the 1980s, it had become increasingly difficult for persons with attention deficits to earn a living. Restaurants have largely been replaced by fast-food "stores" that demand rapid production and strict adherence to standard procedures. Self-service filling stations no longer need human beings to clean the windshield, fill the tank, and check the tires. Auto mechanics must now be expert at computer analysis of modern automobiles. Working in a warehouse now requires the ability to create computer printouts and interpret computer-generated codes. Loading trucks is no longer a simple matter of moving crates and boxes. Complex laws governing child care often make it impossible for women to earn extra income by supervising children in their homes. As our culture approaches the 21st century, the workplace requires higher level computer skills, calm ability to function quickly under pressure, and enough education to qualify for licenses according to government regulations. Adults who have residual-type ADHD or ADD find it very difficult to earn a living. Several million young adults continue to live with their parents because they cannot earn enough to live on their own. Several million American parents are caught in the "sandwich generation," having to care for aging parents while still providing for adult children who cannot manage for themselves. Adults who have residual-type ADHD or ADD swell the ranks of unemployed and underemployed workers in our culture.

ADHD on the Job

Jo's parents held their marriage together in spite of the battering experience of rearing a daughter who had severe ADHD. Until onset of puberty at age 12, Jo was at Level 9 in hyperactivity and lack of self-control. The Barkers survived those difficult years through the help of Ritalin, which brought down Jo's behavior to Level 7 for a few hours each day. Then they endured the evening storms unleashed by rebound as her restrained energy and emotions broke loose about dinner time. Hormone development gradually reduced the force of her hyperactivity to Level 8, then to Level 7 by the time she entered ninth grade. With continued treatment through medication, Jo stayed in school with barely passing grades. Outbursts of dyslogical behavior threatened school failure, but private tutoring and frequent counseling sessions enabled her to graduate with her high school class. Mr. and Mrs. Barker cried with relief as they watched their difficult daughter receive her high school diploma. Surely, they told themselves, we will get a break. After 18 traumatic years, they looked forward to the "empty nest" their friends described. Jo was their only child. They dared not have more children when the severity of her ADHD became clear.

Jo received several hundred dollars as graduation gifts. She talked about using that money to rent her own apartment with a friend. The Barkers encouraged this plan. They helped Jo and her friend look for an apartment they could afford and shop for household things. Three weeks after high school commencement, the Barkers received a telephone call one evening. It was Jo telling them that she was at a summer resort with several friends. On the spur of the moment, they had decided to "party" because they were going separate ways in a few weeks. She would be home sometime. Then she hung up without leaving her number or address. She was gone for 10 days. Late one night a call came from a sheriff's office in a neighboring state. "I'm in jail," Jo said in her old angry voice. "This bunch of jerks arrested me for drunk driving. Come get me out of this crappy place!" Mr. Barker listened to several minutes of her anger; then he got the sheriff's deputy on the line. Jo and some friends had been stopped doing 90 miles per hour in a 45 mile-per-hour speed zone. Jo was driving and immediately began to yell and resist the officer's effort to check things out. The deputy finally determined that she was driving without a license, and she registered .018 on the breath test for intoxication. The legal limit for blood alcohol in that state was .005. Jo faced several hundred dollars in fines. She also needed an attorney to represent her in the local court. This postgraduation party cost the Barkers more than $2,000. All of Jo's gift money had been spent with nothing left for the apartment.

For several weeks following this upset, Jo lived in constant anger toward her parents. "We're back to the days when she was seven before we started Ritalin," Mrs. Barker sobbed one night. Because Jo was 18 years old, her parents could not force her to see a counselor or renew her medication prescription. "I'm a legal adult!" she yelled. "You can't make me anymore!" Relatives and church friends advised the Barkers to practice "tough love" by forcing Jo to leave their house unless she obeyed their rules. Her parents could not bring themselves to take such a drastic step.

By September, Jo began to calm down and become less angry. Her parents realized that her anger was actually a smoke screen to cover her anxiety. In reality, she was deeply afraid of stepping out on her own. She realized that she had no job skills to offer an employer. "I can't do anything right!" she sobbed one night to her mother. "All my life I've screwed everything up! I can't make it on my own without you and Dad. It makes me so mad at myself! I'm nothing but a _____ failure!" Jo finally agreed to talk things over with the only counselor she had ever trusted. The counselor encouraged her to apply for at least a part-time job. They worked out a list of jobs that would not press her too hard. Her ADHD patterns made it very hard for her to follow oral instructions, especially if there was background noise while she listened. Her short attention span caused her to "blink" or "go blank" instead of staying on task. Her lack of organization made it hard for her to keep a workspace tidy. Her poor sense of time meant that she must be reminded when and where to be. As Jo reviewed all of these patterns with her counselor, she decided to look for work. She was too bored and restless to stay at home and watch television all day.

The counselor warned Jo that being turned down for jobs would be her most difficult challenge. "You are a very sensitive person," her counselor reminded her. "You will take it as personal rejection if you are turned down when you apply." This prediction was correct. After being turned down three times by personnel directors, Jo slipped into a state of depression for several days. Her old fear of failure returned heavily, and her lifelong battle with low self-esteem became acute. She cried. She became angry. She began sleeping all day. Finally Mr. Barker asked a friend who owned several ice cream shops to give Jo a job to help her build up her courage. The friend agreed. Jo was to begin work at 3:00 P.M. the following Monday afternoon.

Jo was late to work that first day. As her parents left the house that morning, they reminded her to watch the clock. Mrs. Barker called at noon to remind her again, but this set off an argument over the phone. "I'm not a baby!" Jo yelled at her mother. "Stay off my back!" Then she turned on the television and lost track of time. At 2:50, she saw the clock. She dashed to her car and raced off toward work. She ran out of gas a mile from the house because she had forgotten to fill the tank when her father reminded her the day before. A man she knew brought gas from the filling station and started her car. Then she discovered that she had left her purse and credit cards at home. Back to the house she raced, then rushed to work. She was 20 minutes late and out of breath.

Robb, the manager of the ice cream shop, was irritated by Jo's late arrival. He was already irritated because a friend of the boss had gotten his daughter this job. An impressive young man had applied for the position, but Robb was told to hire Jo instead. So the new job started on a negative note. The manager was impatient when it was clear that this new worker needed everything repeated. If Robb kept on explaining, Jo interrupted, "What do you mean?" Within a few minutes of on-the-job training, the manager was feeling hostile toward this new employee whom he had not wanted in the first place. Jo began to boil inside, as she always did when anyone in authority told her to listen and stop interrupting. Those words always triggered her anger because it made her feel "dumb" to be told to listen better. She tried to hold her temper under control, but as the work session continued, her old ADHD patterns emerged. Before she had been on the job 2 hours, Jo flared into a shouting match with her new manager. Robb reminded her who was boss. Those words were the last straw. "Well, you can take this rotten job and shove it!" she screamed as she stomped out of the shop.

During the next 4 months, Jo was hired, then fired, from seven jobs. Each time, she promised her counselor and parents that she would do better. Each time she started a new job, she fully intended to make this one a success. Each time, she soon reached the point of failure. She worked a few days selling tie-dyed T-shirts in a boutique. She made so many mistakes at the cash register that the boss finally let her go. She found a job making cinnamon pastries in a shopping mall, but this job required her to work in an open space where shoppers could stand and watch. Jo could not keep her attention focused on her work. After spoiling several batches of pastry dough, she was fired for being "careless." Then she found part-time work that sounded exciting. She was to sell cosmetics by telephone. Like most of her friends, Jo loved talking on the phone. This job lasted half a day. She could not remember the sales message she was required to say. Besides, she began to feel angry when several people hung up as she introduced herself by phone. Her love of telephone talking did not give her the right skills for this oral communication.

Then Jo was hired to sell costume jewelry in a department store. All her life she had had a natural talent for fashion. She did well for the first 2 weeks and began to feel confident of her skills. One Friday evening during rush hour, three of her high school friends came by. As they laughed and talked about old times, customers stood in line. Several customers interrupted and asked Jo to help them with purchases. Her old habits of resenting authority emerged, and she said sharply, "Just wait a minute! I'm busy!" Then she returned to gossiping with her friends. A customer complained to the floor manager, who came to see what the problem might be. When the manager told Jo's friends to leave and reminded her that customers were waiting, Jo's lifelong temper flared. Jo walked off yet another job having a tantrum. Later she rationalized to her parents, "I hated that old job anyway. They make you work like a slave and don't pay anything. I won't waste my time at a place like that!"

Three more jobs came and went with similar stories. As Christmas approached, the Barkers realized with heavy hearts how handicapped their daughter was as a young adult with still-active patterns of ADHD. They joined a parent support group called CH.A.D.D., where they shared their sad story with others who were also trapped with adult children who had residual-type ADHD. To their dismay, they learned that many families still support children long after high school. The Barkers learned that our culture is filled by many young adults who have residual-type ADHD. They do not possess workplace skills that fit today's job market. They do not possess the social skills to fit into the adult world successfully. They do not have the emotional maturity to absorb normal social pressures without losing self-control as they did when they were children. These young adults who have residual-type ADHD are children in grown-up bodies. They still need the supervision they required during childhood and adolescence, yet they are too proud, too insecure, and too self-focused to permit parents and other adults to provide supervision. They are demanding in the selfish ways that spoiled relationships when they were young. They are too shallow to comprehend the principle that it is more blessed to give than to receive. They do not express gratitude to parents who are exhausted from all the years of forgiving, providing, and carrying most of the burden within the family. These adults with ADHD cannot establish separate lives. They cannot function successfully on jobs. They cannot stay in personal relationships that require give and take. They are locked into lifestyles that are immature, self-centered, and often destructive. And they refuse the help offered by loved ones, friends, and community. Parents like the Barkers often search in vain for hope that things will soon improve as they wrestle the problems created by their adult children who still have ADHD.

ADD on the Job

Lee finally graduated from high school with the daily help of his parents, older sister, grandmother, and two private tutors. He also had the partial refuge of the school's resource room, where he was under constant supervision in two classes. All his life he had been the most forgetful, most absent-minded person his family had ever known. Through the years, Mr. and Mrs. Hobbs tried every trick in the book to help Lee remember. They covered the refrigerator with stick-on notes reminding him what to do after school, what time to turn on the oven to finish dinner, when to feed and water the dog, and where to be at certain times. Every detail of his life had to be supervised, or else he forgot. After working at their jobs all day, Mr. and Mrs. Hobbs faced the task of rounding up Lee's schoolbooks for homework. They usually had to dash back to school to get something he had forgotten to bring home. They often had to go to the bus barn to retrieve something he had left on the bus. They lost track of how many new jackets, caps, gloves, and even socks he lost during his years in school. Without adult supervision, Lee could not finish anything he started. The attic was filled with half-finished models of all kinds. His room was littered with half-finished projects and posters he abandoned. His locker at school was stuffed with paper that represented half-finished homework never turned in. After dragging him through assignments at night, Mr. and Mrs. Hobbs wore themselves out reminding Lee to get all of his schoolwork into his book bag. He usually left something important behind as he ran to catch the bus. The orthodontist complained about Lee's failure to care for his teeth and braces. The eye doctor could not believe how many times he had replaced the glasses Lee needed for school. Now this loose, poorly organized young man was ready to find a job and get on with becoming an adult. Lee's ADD patterns had diminished during adolescence. At age 11, he was at Level 8 on the severity scale. By age 14, he was down to Level 7. At age 18, he was about Level 6. But he was still "loose as a goose," as his grandmother expressed it.

In every situation, Lee's good sense of humor saved the day. No one could stay angry with him very long. He never seemed upset. He was always glad to see others, even when they scolded him for being so forgetful and inattentive. His kind behavior made quick friends everywhere he went. The fact that he was always rumpled and needed to comb his hair did not take away from his grin and friendly attitude. When he forgot to shower and use deodorant for several days, others overlooked his poor grooming. "Wow! That kid sure is ripe!" his Grandpa said every now and then. But Grandpa still bragged on this grandson to everyone who would listen.

Lee fully intended to go to college, but high school graduation was over and he had not gotten around to applying for college admission. He had forgotten to show up for the college admission test that was required by all of the state colleges. He began looking for a job the week after graduation. Within 2 days, he was hired to deliver floral arrangements for a local florist. The owner of the floral shop was charmed by this young man's smile and friendly attitude. Part of Lee's responsibility was to take inventory of cut flowers and potted plants every Tuesday and Thursday afternoons. Keeping enough flowers on hand depended on those inventories. Lee could read well and had no trouble handling numbers. But as he hurried from work that first Tuesday to go fishing with his grandfather, he forgot to take the inventory. Two unexpected funerals occurred on Wednesday, and the shop ran out of flowers. The florist listened to Lee's apology. "Well, I will forgive it this time," the manager said, "but don't let it happen again. We just can't stay in business if we don't keep track of our inventory." Two weeks later Lee forgot again. This time the manager fired him. "You're one of the nicest boys I've ever had here," the florist said. "But, Lee, you have cost me $500. I have to let you go."

It did not take Lee long to find another job. This time he was hired as night-shift cashier in a prepay self-service filling station. He was locked inside a glass booth with bulletproof windows. His job was to take money or credit cards before the customers filled their tanks. He had to watch all the cars that pulled up to the 16 gasoline pumps. He was to stop any pump immediately if the driver tried to fill his tank before paying in advance at Lee's window. The third night on the job, a lull came in traffic. Ten minutes went by with no customers, so Lee started to read a book. Soon he was lost in the story. He did not see four cars pull up to the pumps that were farthest from his booth. These drivers knew how to activate the pumps without paying in advance. They filled their tanks, then slipped away without Lee seeing them. The next day, he was fired and had to pay the filling station owner for the stolen gas.

During the next 2 years, Lee was fired from more than 20 jobs. His mother kept a log of her son's job history. "Someday when I write my book," she said many times, "people will not believe it." Lee lost jobs because he was late too many times. No matter how many alarm clocks went off beside his bed, he could not wake up without a struggle. He lost several more jobs because he forgot to do essential tasks. He was fired for wearing soiled uniforms after being warned to make sure he was fresh and clean. Twice he lost his job because he loaded merchandise on the wrong trucks. He had been watching something down the dock and did not notice what he was doing. Lee could not keep track of work schedules unless he was reminded. He lost several jobs because he failed to notice changes for his shift. Three times he was fined for losing important papers on the job. He was forever being nagged for having too much clutter in his workspace. Managers fussed at him constantly for failing to put equipment away before leaving his shift. Yet every time he was fired, Lee was told, "You're one of the nicest guys we've ever had work here, but I have to let you go." This nice guy who had Level 6 ADD could not cope successfully with workplace expectations.

When Lee was 21 years old, he was still living at home with his parents. They continued to help him make car payments and pay his bills. Finally, he met a girl and fell in love. Mr. and Mrs. Hobbs were delighted with Nancy. "That girl has common sense," said Mr. Hobbs as they watched her reason with Lee. Nancy was able to give advice in a way that did not offend or embarrass him. She began helping him notice that he needed to improve his appearance. On Saturdays they went shopping, where Nancy taught Lee how to pay attention to clothes and styles. She suggested that he let her help him keep track of how he spent his money. Then she showed him how to keep track of time by using a folding calendar that fit into his pocket. Nancy coached Lee in watching clocks wherever he happened to be. She helped him understand why it is important not to start reading a book on the job or make too many phone calls while he was at work. By the time Nancy and Lee announced their engagement to be married, he was holding the first steady job he had had since high school. By letting Nancy become his supervisor, Lee learned to compensate for his residual ADD. As his mother wrote years later in her book about rearing a son with ADD, "The key to success for anyone who has ADD is finding a supervisor. Children who have ADD need supervision. Teens must have supervision, although they rebel against it. Adults who still have ADD also need good supervisors. My son became a successful man when he had the good sense to marry the most wonderful supervisor in the world."

3

HOW TO HELP INDIVIDUALS WHO HAVE ADHD AND ADD

Major Interventions

In Chapters 1 and 2, we saw what happens when no one intervenes to help those who struggle with the disruptive patterns of ADHD and ADD. Persons who live with ADHD or ADD are often helpless to do better or to correct mistakes unless they receive outside help. Yet it is often hard for these persons to accept the help they need. In Chapter 1, we reviewed the checklist of ADHD and ADD behaviors. We also looked at the severity scale along which ADHD and ADD behaviors range from mild to severe. As we saw in the story of James in Chapter 2, it was virtually impossible for his parents and professionals to intervene because of his intense anger toward those who tried to manage his behavior. We read the story of Jo, whose ADHD tendencies caused her to reject the help she desperately needed to be successful. Providing necessary intervention is not always easy. Sometimes it is impossible. As parents, counselors, teachers, and therapists, we often find that our efforts to help are blocked by angry resistance. However, if persons who have ADHD or ADD behavior at the high end of the severity scale are to succeed, they must be willing to accept some type of intervention, or they face many years of failure at school, at home, and on the job.

I met Phil at a professional conference where I conducted an all-day seminar about ADHD and ADD. Sitting in the front row directly before me was this handsome man who was well dressed and obviously bright. Before I began my presentation, Phil introduced himself and chatted for a few minutes. He told me that he was 43 years old, was working on his doctoral degree in psychology, was director of an adult education agency where high school dropouts could finish their GED preparation, and was on the governor's commission to study the problems of illiteracy in his state. Although Phil made a good impression as he presented himself to me, something caused me to wonder. Why was such an articulate, poised man still working on his doctorate at age 43? I noticed as I spoke that Phil soaked up every word I said about ADHD and ADD. He was fascinated by the map of the brain I used to show slow blood flow and low sugar metabolism in persons who have dyslexia and attention deficit patterns. He listened intently to the questions and answers during group discussion. Following this presentation about the causes, behaviors, and consequences of ADHD and ADD, Phil followed me to my car. Then I learned the truth about this intelligent man.

On the outside, Phil appears successful. He has all the appearance of being a high achiever. In reality, he is a failure. This unhappy man is trapped in lifelong cycles of failure that he cannot break. He told me that he is alcoholic but has been sober for 6 years through constant attendance at Alcoholics Anonymous meetings. He follows the AA 12-step recovery program with his sponsor. He was married long enough to have children, but his wife left him in despair when it became clear that he was not going to get his life under control. He knows that he has severe reactive hypoglycemia that sends him every afternoon into downward spirals of energy loss, yet he cannot stay on any kind of diet to control blood sugar levels. He smoked five packs of cigarettes per day most of his adult life. He quit smoking at age 38 when he almost died from pneumonia. Phil's mind is never at rest. His head spins with intelligent, creative ideas and concepts. Yet he has never finished anything he has started. "My life is like a garbage dump," he said. "I leave behind me trails of good things I start but never finish. I can't hold a job. I can't make good grades in school. I can't discipline myself to study and finish graduate school. I alienate everyone who is kind to me. I am a con artist, and I manipulate everyone I meet. Right now I am trying to con you into helping me think well of myself. A few years ago I scored 150 IQ on the Wechsler Intelligence Test, yet I feel so dumb and stupid. I know I need help, but

I have never let anyone get close enough to me to give me the help I need. Now I am truly desperate. What can I do? Where can I go for help?''

There are many thousands of adults like Phil in our society. They drift. They float. They start but never finish. They have great potential that is never developed. They con. They manipulate. They find themselves lying, cheating, even stealing. They can quote sermons, scripture, and lectures on being good and working hard and overcoming weakness. They continually go to meetings and seminars and workshops to learn more about themselves and their problems. They follow specialists to their cars and bombard them with questions. But nothing changes for these strugglers who live with chronic failure. The missing piece to their puzzle is that they do not allow helpers to intervene with strategies that could change their lives. All of the Phils we meet frustrate us. They break our hearts. They stay just beyond our reach until they come to the point of being ready to accept intervention. Phil finally gave up smoking when his life was in mortal danger. He eventually turned to Alcoholics Anonymous when he saw that he could not survive if he continued to abuse alcohol. He became so ill he submitted to the 6-hour glucose tolerance test and slipped into hypoglycemic shock when his blood sugar dropped to a critical level. This revealed his body chemistry imbalance that sabotages his mental and physical energy every day. With his extraordinary intelligence, Phil knows what he needs to do, but he is not yet ready to trust others. He cannot permit an outsider to intervene through medical supervision, including strict diet control. Until he is ready to take that step, all of his strengths will be canceled by the weaknesses that overwhelm his good intentions to get his life under control.

Before we look at specific kinds of intervention that help most persons with ADHD and ADD, we must consider a factor that plays a critical role in how we intervene. For several years, those of us who work with persons who have ADHD and ADD have talked about the issue of *arousal.* The concept of arousal refers to brain activity. Persons who have normally developed neuronal pathways and brain structures go through regular cycles of arousal. At certain times, the body rhythms slow down, allowing us to become calm, relax, and sleep soundly. As the level of arousal decreases, all body functions slow down and become less active. This ability to rest is often called repose. The ability to find repose means that we can turn loose, ''parachute down,'' and let ourselves relax without keeping ourselves aroused and on guard. In the same way, persons who have normally developed brain structures and normal body chemistry are able to turn their attention away from rest and become ready for work. The person's body systems become alert with higher levels of blood flow and increased sugar metabolism. As arousal increases, we think more clearly, pay attention to tasks more energetically, and burn up energy more rapidly. Emotions awaken. Body functions become alert. Energy soars and arouses us to become more active. Mental activity increases so that the brain is metabolizing sugar more rapidly and in greater quantities. Adrenalin flow increases. Digestive activity becomes more rapid and intense. All of the body and mind are on alert during arousal. At the appropriate time, the arousal cycle slows down and we turn again toward rest and repose. For most people, these cycles of arousal and rest are automatic, controlled, and regular. However, arousal and rest are not regular or automatic in persons who have ADHD and ADD.

In Chapter 1, we reviewed recent discoveries about the causes of ADHD and ADD. We now know that portions of the cerebellum are immature, causing lack of organization and poor impulse control (Denckla, 1991). We know that blood supply in certain areas of the left brain is too low. Blood flow is too slow to give the brain a steady supply of fuel (glucose). This inadequate glucose metabolism in the brain triggers all kinds of ADHD and ADD reactions (Anastopoulos & Barkley, 1991; Zametkin, 1991). As this kind of research continues, we will become aware of even more details about faulty brain chemistry, heredity, and body chemistry that interfere with normal cycles of arousal and rest. When the body cannot develop or maintain regular cycles of resting and being active, it is impossible for the person to fit into his or her world successfully.

As we look at ways to help individuals who have ADHD and ADD, we must again refer to the severity scale shown in Chapters 1 and 2:

0	1 2 3	4 5 6 7	8 9 10
none	mild	moderate	severe

We do not need to intervene when ADHD and ADD symptoms are at a moderate level, other than to offer occasional advice and remind the person to check his or her schedule. Individuals who have ADHD and ADD below Level 5 usually manage on their own reasonably well. Intervention becomes important when ADHD or ADD is at Level 6 or 7. The person must have help to stay on schedule, finish tasks, do necessary chores, and follow the rules at work or at school. Intervention becomes critical when ADHD or ADD patterns are severe. Persons at Level 8, 9, or 10 cannot function on their own.

When Do We Intervene?

Some of the wisest advice about how to manage ADHD and ADD comes from Martha Denckla, who is directing magnetic resonance imaging (MRI) studies at Johns Hopkins School of Medicine. For several years, Denckla and her staff have studied cerebellar structures in children and adolescents who have attention deficit struggles. Most of these students have fallen through the cracks of psychometric assessment that is based upon standardized test scores. In 1984, most states adopted what is called criteria learning disability (CLD) assessment procedures. For a student to be classified as having a learning disability, he or she must show severe discrepancy between ability (IQ) and academic skills. To be recognized as having a learning disability, a student must have a 15-point difference or more between the Full Scale IQ score on the *Wechsler Intelligence Scale for Children–Revised* (WISC–R) or the *Wechsler Adult Intelligence Scale–Revised* (WAIS–R) and standard scores on such tests as the *Woodcock–Johnson Psycho-Educational Battery.* Each state sets its own score discrepancy range. Some states require a 15-point difference between Wechsler scores and standard scores from achievement tests. Other states may require a 20-point discrepancy or higher. This method of looking for learning disability does not categorize students using specific terminology such as "dyslexia" or "attention deficit disorder." When score discrepancy is the method used, the only students who are labeled learning disabled are those whose scores show a wide enough difference between IQ score and academic skill scores.

As we will see in Chapter 4, many professionals are challenging this narrow view of learning struggle. Denckla is leading the way toward a broader professional approach to intervention on behalf of those who struggle with attention deficit patterns. She has proposed the concept of *Executive Function* (Denckla, 1991). This means that instead of looking at scores from tests, we should analyze how well persons function in three areas: attention, organization, and inhibition. By analyzing how well or how poorly an individual manages his or her attention, organizes his or her life, and controls impulses, we see much more clearly when and how to intervene. Scores from standardized tests cannot give us this kind of vital information.

The Jordan Executive Function Index for Children. The following pages present the *Jordan Executive Function Index for Children.* Parents are asked to fill out the Parent Response page, along with the following three pages of questions titled Attention, Organization, and Inhibition. A teacher who knows the child well is asked to complete the Teacher Response questionnaire, as well as the following three pages of questions titled Attention, Organization, and Inhibition. The purpose of the *Jordan Executive Function Index* is to pull together the behaviors that upset the family, interfere with classroom learning, and disrupt social activity. By finding the level of severity of the child's behavior, we see how much intervention must be done to help this person become successful at school, at home, and in the community.

JORDAN EXECUTIVE FUNCTION INDEX FOR CHILDREN

PARENT RESPONSE

Name _____ Date _____ _____ _____
                                      year   month   day

Grade _____ Retained? ___ ___ Birthdate _____ _____ _____
                        yes no   year   month   day

If retained, what year? _____ Age _____ _____ _____
                                        year   month   day

Adopted? ___ ___
         yes no

Speech Development ___ ___ ___ Tooth Development ___ ___ ___
                  early on time late   early on time late

Allergies _____ _____ _____ _____ Otitis Media ___ ___
          none   mild   moderate severe   yes no

Mother's Pregnancy _____ _____ _____
                   normal   difficult some problems off and on

Birth Length _____ Birth Weight _____ _____
             inches   pounds ounces

Born Early? ___ ___ If early, how early? _____
            yes no

**On the next three pages, please mark the item before each
statement that is MOST like this student MOST of the time.**

Never 0	Sometimes 1	Usually 2	Always 3	**ATTENTION**
				Keeps attention focused on the task without darting/drifting off on mental rabbit trails.
				Tunes out (ignores) what goes on nearby in order to keep on doing necessary tasks.
				Keeps on listening to oral information without darting/drifting off on mental rabbit trails.
				Listens to new information, understands it without saying, "Huh?" or "What?" or "What do you mean?"
				Finishes tasks without wandering off on rabbit trails before work is completed.
				Does necessary tasks without needing continual reminding and supervision.
				Can be part of a team or play group without wandering off on mental rabbit trails during the game.
				Follows the rules of games without having to be reminded over and over.
				Can take part in group activities without being called back to attention over and over.
				Remembers what to do after school without being reminded/supervised.
				Remembers phone messages and messages from teachers to parents.
				Cleans up own room/workspace without supervision.
				Does routine chores without being reminded and supervised.
				Pays attention to TV shows/movies without wandering off on mental rabbit trails.
				Notices how others respond to his/her behavior. Picks up cues as to how own behavior should be changed.
				Notices details (how things are alike/different) without being told to notice.
				Notices how/where objects are placed and tries not to bump/knock them over.
				Notices how work pages are organized (how lines are numbered, how details are spaced, where written responses should go).
				Follows conversations without losing it or jumping to a different subject before others finish speaking.

Add all of the scores: 0 for Never, 1 for Sometimes, 2 for Usually, 3 for Always

TOTAL SCORE _____

Never 0	Sometimes 1	Usually 2	Always 3	ORGANIZATION
				Keeps track of own things without losing them.
				Gathers up things and gets them back to school without having to be reminded/ supervised.
				Keeps track of assignments/school projects without having to be reminded/supervised.
				Keeps room/desk/locker clean and orderly without supervision.
				Keeps clothes/personal belongings organized without being told/supervised.
				Keeps work space orderly while doing tasks.
				Hears or reads instructions, then does the task in an orderly way without supervision.
				Plays with things, then puts them away without being supervised.
				Works with tools/materials, then cleans up/puts them away without being supervised.
				Spaces written work well on page without having to do it again.
				Plans ahead/budgets time realistically without needing supervision.
				Has realistic sense of time without needing reminding/supervision.
				Manages own money realistically without supervision.
				Plans activities, then explains plans to others without help.
				Plans ahead for gifts at Christmas/Hanukkah/ birthdays without help.
				Notices sequence patterns (how things should be arranged) without being told.
				Keeps things together in appropriate groups (books on shelves, school papers together, shoes in pairs, tools in sets, knives/forks/spoons in correct place) without being reminded/supervised.
				Keeps schoolwork organized in notebooks, folders, files, stacks without supervision.
				Plays by the rules. Wants playmates/teammates to follow the rules.
				Does tasks in order from start to finish without skipping around.

Add all of the scores: 0 for Never, 1 for Sometimes, 2 for Usually, 3 for Always

TOTAL SCORE _____

Never 0	Sometimes 1	Usually 2	Always 3	**INHIBITION**
				Thinks of consequences before doing what comes to mind.
				Puts off pleasure in order to finish necessary work.
				Follows own sense of right and wrong instead of being influenced by others.
				Puts needs and welfare of others ahead of own wishes/desires.
				Says "no" to own impulses when responsibilities must be carried out.
				Makes an effort to grow up instead of remaining immature or impulsive.
				Tries to change habits/mannerisms that bother/offend others.
				Learns from experience. Thinks about lessons learned the hard way.
				Lives by rules/spiritual principles instead of by whim/impulse.
				Accepts responsibility instead of making excuses/blaming others.
				Asks for help/advice instead of being stubborn.
				Apologizes/asks forgiveness when behavior has hurt/offended others.
				Is recognized by peers and leaders as being mature, unselfish, dependable, teachable, cooperative.
				Stops inappropriate impulses/desires before they emerge so that others will not be bothered/offended.
				Sticks to promises/agreements without being reminded or supervised.
				Goes the extra mile for others without complaining or feeling self-pity.
				Sets long-term goals and works toward them without complaining or quitting.
				Absorbs teasing/rudeness without flaring or becoming defensive.
				Is kind toward others. Avoids sarcasm/hateful remarks/putdowns.
				Resists urge to take things apart, tear structures down, rip things apart, pick at things with fingers.
				Is flexible and creative instead of being ritualized and rigid.

Add all of the scores: 0 for Never, 1 for Sometimes, 2 for Usually, 3 for Always

TOTAL SCORE _____

JORDAN EXECUTIVE FUNCTION INDEX FOR CHILDREN

TEACHER RESPONSE

Name _____   Date _____ _____ _____
                                       year   month   day

Grade _____   Retained? ___ ___   Birthdate _____ _____ _____
                          yes no   year   month   day

If retained, what year? _____   Age _____ _____ _____
                                        year   month   day

CLASSROOM PERFORMANCE

High Achiever	Average Achiever	Low Achiever
No Struggle	Moderate Struggle	Severe Struggle
High Motivation (always motivated)	Average Motivation (comes and goes)	Low Motivation (seldom motivated)
Fits in well. Liked by peers. Little or no peer conflict.	Some conflict. Not always liked by peers. Usually fits in with adult guidance.	Continual conflict. Disliked by peers. Can't fit in even with adult guidance.
Usually cheerful and happy.	Often moody, touchy, grouchy, irritable.	Seldom cheerful. Usually unhappy. Overly sensitive and touchy.
Outgoing. Active. Eager to cooperate. Ready to lead.	Quiet, passive. Willing to follow and cooperate.	Withdrawn. Does not want to cooperate or participate. Unconnected from group.

On the next three pages, please mark the item before each statement that is MOST like this student MOST of the time.

Never 0	Sometimes 1	Usually 2	Always 3	**ATTENTION**
				Keeps attention focused on the task without darting/drifting off on mental rabbit trails.
				Tunes out (ignores) what goes on nearby in order to keep on doing necessary tasks.
				Keeps on listening to oral information without darting/drifting off on mental rabbit trails.
				Listens to new information, understands it without saying, "Huh?" or "What?" or "What do you mean?"
				Finishes tasks without wandering off on rabbit trails before work is completed.
				Does necessary tasks without needing continual reminding and supervision.
				Can be part of a team or play group without wandering off on mental rabbit trails during the game.
				Follows the rules of games without having to be reminded over and over.
				Can take part in group activities without being called back to attention over and over.
				Remembers what to do after school without being reminded/supervised.
				Remembers phone messages and messages from teachers to parents.
				Cleans up own room/workspace without supervision.
				Does routine chores without being reminded and supervised.
				Pays attention to TV shows/movies without wandering off on mental rabbit trails.
				Notices how others respond to his/her behavior. Picks up cues as to how own behavior should be changed.
				Notices details (how things are alike/different) without being told to notice.
				Notices how/where objects are placed and tries not to bump/knock them over.
				Notices how work pages are organized (how lines are numbered, how details are spaced, where written responses should go).
				Follows conversations without losing it or jumping to a different subject before others finish speaking.

Add all of the scores: 0 for Never, 1 for Sometimes, 2 for Usually, 3 for Always

TOTAL SCORE _____

Never 0	Sometimes 1	Usually 2	Always 3	**ORGANIZATION**
				Keeps track of own things without losing them.
				Gathers up things and gets them back to school without having to be reminded/supervised.
				Keeps track of assignments/school projects without having to be reminded/supervised.
				Keeps room/desk/locker clean and orderly without supervision.
				Keeps clothes/personal belongings organized without being told/supervised.
				Keeps work space orderly while doing tasks.
				Hears or reads instructions, then does the task in an orderly way without supervision.
				Plays with things, then puts them away without being supervised.
				Works with tools/materials, then cleans up/puts them away without being supervised.
				Spaces written work well on page without having to do it again.
				Plans ahead/budgets time realistically without needing supervision.
				Has realistic sense of time without needing reminding/supervision.
				Manages own money realistically without supervision.
				Plans activities, then explains plans to others without help.
				Plans ahead for gifts at Christmas/Hanukkah/birthdays without help.
				Notices sequence patterns (how things should be arranged) without being told.
				Keeps things together in appropriate groups (books on shelves, school papers together, shoes in pairs, tools in sets, knives/forks/spoons in correct place) without being reminded/supervised.
				Keeps schoolwork organized in notebooks, folders, files, stacks without supervision.
				Plays by the rules. Wants playmates/teammates to follow the rules.
				Does tasks in order from start to finish without skipping around.

Add all of the scores: 0 for Never, 1 for Sometimes, 2 for Usually, 3 for Always

TOTAL SCORE _____

Never 0	Sometimes 1	Usually 2	Always 3	INHIBITION
				Thinks of consequences before doing what comes to mind.
				Puts off pleasure in order to finish necessary work.
				Follows own sense of right and wrong instead of being influenced by others.
				Puts needs and welfare of others ahead of own wishes/desires.
				Says "no" to own impulses when responsibilities must be carried out.
				Makes an effort to grow up instead of remaining immature or impulsive.
				Tries to change habits/mannerisms that bother/offend others.
				Learns from experience. Thinks about lessons learned the hard way.
				Lives by rules/spiritual principles instead of by whim/impulse.
				Accepts responsibility instead of making excuses/blaming others.
				Asks for help/advice instead of being stubborn.
				Apologizes/asks forgiveness when behavior has hurt/offended others.
				Is recognized by peers and leaders as being mature, unselfish, dependable, teachable, cooperative.
				Stops inappropriate impulses/desires before they emerge so that others will not be bothered/offended.
				Sticks to promises/agreements without being reminded or supervised.
				Goes the extra mile for others without complaining or feeling self-pity.
				Sets long-term goals and works toward them without complaining or quitting.
				Absorbs teasing/rudeness without flaring or becoming defensive.
				Is kind toward others. Avoids sarcasm/hateful remarks/putdowns.
				Resists urge to take things apart, tear structures down, rip things apart, pick at things with fingers.
				Is flexible and creative instead of being ritualized and rigid.

Add all of the scores: 0 for Never, 1 for Sometimes, 2 for Usually, 3 for Always

TOTAL SCORE _____

Rating Scale.   To determine whether intervention is needed and to tell what kinds of intervention will be helpful, the Total Scores from the Attention, Organization, and Inhibition sections of the Parent Response form are added to the Total Scores from the respective sections of the Teacher Response form. Then these new Total Scores for Attention, Organization, and Inhibition are divided by 2. If two teachers fill out questionnaires, then three Total Scores are added and divided by 3. The new averaged Total Scores are now the Final Score, which is written on the Summary of Behaviors, on the following pages.

For example, James's parents completed their Parent Response form. Their checkmarks gave him a Total Score of 8 for Attention. The teacher gave him a Total Score of 6 for Attention. These two scores are added (14), and then divided by 2 to obtain James's Final Score of 7 for Attention. His Parent Response score for Organization is 5 and his Teacher Response score is 7, giving a Final Score for Organization of 6. His Parent Response score is 4 for Inhibition, and his Teacher Response score is 6, giving a Final Score for Inhibition of 5.

These Final Scores are now transferred to the Summary of Behaviors on the following pages. James's Final Score of 6 for Attention ranks him at the Severe Attention Deficit level. His Final Score of 7 for Organization ranks him at the Severe Organizational Deficit level. His Final Score of 5 for Inhibition ranks him at the Severe Problems with Self-Control level.

JORDAN EXECUTIVE FUNCTION INDEX FOR CHILDREN

SUMMARY OF BEHAVIORS

Rating Scale

0 to 11	12 to 25	26 to 40	41 to 55	56 to 60
severe	moderately severe	moderate	mild	none

FINAL SCORE   ATTENTION SUMMARY

_____ 0–11 **Severe Attention Deficit**
Cannot function in mainstream classroom or group. Must have constant supervision to succeed. Cannot do sustained tasks without one-to-one monitoring. Cannot follow instructions without step-by-step supervision. Very short work time. Loses the task (off on rabbit trails) after 40 to 90 seconds.

Medication and diet control will probably be required before this student can function in academic and social situations.

_____ 12–25 **Moderately Severe Attention Deficit**
Can function part-time in nonacademic classrooms and groups (activity classes, art, music, crafts) if level of stimulus is controlled. Must have continual supervision to succeed. Can work briefly (2 to 4 minutes) in sustained tasks, but reaches rapid burnout. Can follow simple one-step instructions with continual reminding and supervision. Must have one-to-one instruction to fill in gaps in skills and new information. Must be told and reminded to notice.

Medication and diet control should be considered to help this student succeed and earn praise.

_____ 26–40 **Moderate Attention Deficit**
Can function in mainstream classroom and groups with frequent reminding/supervision. Easily distracted. Wanders off on rabbit trails and must be called back to the task. Must have frequent one-to-one help to fill gaps in skills and new information. Must be guided in following through on instructions. Notices now and then, but needs a lot of reminding to notice and pay attention.

_____ 41–55 **Mild Attention Deficit**
Can function effectively in most situations. Occasionally becomes overly distracted by nearby events. Needs frequent monitoring to finish tasks and stay on schedules. Can be taught to monitor self and bring own attention back to task.

_____ 56–60 **No Attention Deficit**

FINAL SCORE   ORGANIZATION SUMMARY

_____ 0–11   **Severe Organizational Deficit**
Cannot manage own things without help and supervision. Cannot remember where things are, what things are needed for certain tasks, where things were put when last used. Cannot gather up own things without supervision. Cannot remember what to take home or what to bring back to school. Loses things on school bus, at home, in the classroom, in lunchroom, on playground. Loses clothes, books, bookbag, shoes, jackets, wraps. Cannot recall where they were left. Leaves tools and playthings in yard overnight. Cannot clean up own room without direct supervision.

Must be guided/supervised/monitored in order to finish any task. Often called "lazy" and "careless." In continual conflict with adults who do not understand organizational deficits.

_____ 12–25   **Moderately Severe Organizational Deficit**
Must have supervision and help to organize. Can do better if steps are written on notes. Must be reminded to go back to notes/outlines to make sure everything has been finished. Cannot clean up room or do chores without supervision. Cannot manage school things without being reminded. Can learn to follow check-lists and outlines if adults maintain supervision and continue to remind.

Must not be expected to organize or stay on schedule without help.

_____ 26–40   **Moderate Organizational Deficit**
Ability to organize is spotty and unpredictable. Needs a lot of reminding and supervision. Responds well to written reminders (notes, outlines). Must be reminded to refer back to notes and outlines to make sure each step has been followed. Tends to be absentminded. Tends to mislay things. Keeps things in loose piles or stacks that often become mixed together. Must have help cleaning out desk/locker/work space. Has cycles of better organization/poorer organization.

_____ 41–55   **Mild Organizational Deficit**
Can develop effective strategies for staying organized and on schedule. Responds well to keeping calendars, outlines of tasks, schedules on paper. Needs to be reminded frequently. Tends to wander off on rabbit trails and forget. Appears to be absent-minded and careless.

_____ 56–60   **No Organizational Deficit**

FINAL SCORE   INHIBITION SUMMARY

_____ 0–11   **Severe Problems with Self-Control**
Cannot function successfully in relationships. Severely self-focused
and self-centered. Does not notice the needs or wishes of others.
Places self first. Thinks mostly of satisfying own desires. All of personal energy goes toward fulfilling own self-needs. Does not extend
affection without demanding something in return. Cannot respond
normally to the give-and-take of friendships/family relationships/
social relationships. Is irritable, quick tempered, judgmental
when pressed to pay attention to others. Attitude is demanding,
short tempered, critical of others. Refuses to share. Demands to
be first. Wants biggest piece or share for self. Makes insatiable
demands on others. Burns others out. Is often rejected by others.
Moves from one friend to the next after short term of friendship.
Cannot share space peacefully. Usually creates conflict with
others. Cannot fit into groups. Tends to be unhappy much of the
time. Complains, gripes, finds faults when others see no problem.

This person creates continual conflicts for leaders. Must be
handled firmly. Cannot respond to normal suggestions that
depend upon noticing others. Continually argues, challenges
authority, blames others, indulges in self-pity. Uses others
without showing regret or concern.

_____ 12–26   **Moderately Severe Problems with Self-Control**
Has trouble functioning in relationships, but can do so if others
are patient and forgiving enough. Must be closely supervised in
groups. Triggers frequent arguments/conflicts with peers. Is disliked by certain leaders. Is often rejected by peers and/or adults.
Can respond to coaching in how to treat others more kindly, but
such lessons do not last. Does not have a natural bent for
extending kindness and attention to others.

Leaders must intervene frequently to stop conflict or restore
peace. This student requires extra effort from leaders to keep
things going smoothly. This person triggers a lot of dislike from
peers. A lot of his/her time is spent planning revenge and trying
to get even.

_____ 27–41   **Moderate Problems with Self-Control**
Responds to reminding about manners and appropriate behavior.
Requires frequent one-to-one guidance in how to behave more
appropriately and less selfishly. Can respond well to reminder
cues. Responds to guidance/counseling strategies that teach this
person how to notice others. Triggers some conflict within group.
Has good days/bad days in relationships. Argues a lot over trivial
issues. Tends to split hairs over things others take in stride. Is seldom a fully cooperative member of group. Seeks subtle ways to
get even with others.

_____ 42–55 **Mild Problems with Self-Control**
Needs frequent reminding about how to interact with others.
Responds to guidance about noticing needs/wishes of others. Can
learn to put own needs last or postpone wishes until later. Has
good day/bad day cycles in relationships. Needs a lot of
forgiveness and forgiving.

_____ 56–61 **No Problems with Self-Control**

NOTES

The Jordan Executive Function Index for Adults.   The following pages present the *Jordan Executive Function Index for Adults.* The scoring procedure is the same as that used for the children's index. The outcome of this study of an individual shows the level of severity of the person's struggle with attention, organization, and inhibition. As Denckla's (1991) research has shown, these vital life skills are influenced by how maturely the cerebellum does its work. As we have seen, the factors of slow blood flow, restricted blood supply, and rate of brain sugar metabolism directly influence the individual's ability to function independently without needing outside supervision or intervention.

JORDAN EXECUTIVE FUNCTION INDEX FOR ADULTS

LIFE BACKGROUND INFORMATION

Name _____ Date _____ _____ _____
                                         year   month   day

Grade _____ Retained? ___ ___ Birthdate _____ _____ _____
                        yes no   year   month   day

If retained, what year? _____ Age _____ _____ _____
                                         year   month   day

Adopted? ___ ___ Diagnosed as dyslexic? ___ ___ What age? _____
        yes no   yes no

Speech Development ___ _____ ___ Tooth Development ___ _____ ___
                  early on time late   early on time late

Allergies _____ _____ _____ _____ Otitis Media ___ ___
         none   mild   moderate severe   yes no

Mother's Pregnancy _____ _____ _____
                      normal   difficult   some problems off and on

Birth Length _____ Birth Weight _____ _____
             inches   pounds ounces

Born Early? ___ ___ If early, how early? _____
           yes no

Born Late? ___ ___ If late, how late? _____
          yes no

Diagnosed as ADHD? ___ ___ What age? _____ Medication? _____
                  yes no

Diagnosed as ADD? ___ ___ What age? _____ Medication? _____
                 yes no

**On the next three pages, please mark the item before each
statement that is MOST like you MOST of the time.**

Never 0	Sometimes 1	Usually 2	Always 3	ATTENTION
				Keeps attention focused on the task without darting/drifting off on mental rabbit trails.
				Tunes out (ignores) what goes on nearby in order to keep on doing necessary tasks.
				Keeps on listening to oral information without darting/drifting off on mental rabbit trails.
				Listens to new information, understands it without saying, "Huh?" or "What?" or "What do you mean?"
				Finishes tasks without wandering off on rabbit trails before work is completed.
				Does necessary tasks without needing continual reminding and supervision.
				Can be part of a team or group without wandering off on mental rabbit trails during group activity.
				Follows the rules of games without having to be reminded.
				Can take part in group activities without being called back to attention.
				Remembers what to do after work without being reminded/supervised.
				Remembers phone messages.
				Cleans up own room/workspace without being reminded.
				Does routine chores without being reminded.
				Pays attention to TV shows/movies without wandering off on mental rabbit trails.
				Notices how others respond to his/her behavior. Picks up cues as to how own behavior should be changed.
				Notices details (how things are alike/different) without being told to notice.
				Notices how/where objects are placed and tries not to bump/knock them over.
				Notices how work pages are organized (how lines are numbered, how details are spaced, where written responses should go).
				Follows conversations without losing it or jumping to a different subject before others finish speaking.

Add all of the scores: 0 for Never, 1 for Sometimes, 2 for Usually, 3 for Always

TOTAL SCORE _____

Never 0	Sometimes 1	Usually 2	Always 3	ORGANIZATION
				Keeps track of own things without losing them.
				Gathers up things and gets them back to correct places without having to be reminded.
				Keeps track of assignments/work projects without having to be reminded/supervised.
				Keeps room/desk clean and orderly without being reminded.
				Keeps clothes/personal belongings organized without being reminded.
				Keeps work space orderly while doing tasks.
				Hears or reads instructions, then does the task in an orderly way without supervision.
				Gets things out, then puts them away without being supervised.
				Works with tools/materials, then cleans up/puts them away without being supervised.
				Spaces written work well on page without crowding or making messy.
				Plans ahead/budgets time realistically without needing reminders.
				Has realistic sense of time without needing reminding/assistance.
				Manages own money realistically without help.
				Plans activities, then explains plans to others without help.
				Plans ahead for gifts at Christmas/Hanukkah/birthdays without help.
				Notices sequence patterns (how things should be arranged) without being told.
				Keeps things together in appropriate groups (books on shelves, papers together, shoes in pairs, tools in sets, knives/forks/spoons in correct place) without being reminded/supervised.
				Keeps papers organized in notebooks, folders, files, stacks without supervision.
				Plays by the rules. Wants teammates to follow the rules.
				Does tasks in order from start to finish without skipping around.

Add all of the scores: 0 for Never, 1 for Sometimes, 2 for Usually, 3 for Always

TOTAL SCORE _____

Never 0	Sometimes 1	Usually 2	Always 3	**INHIBITION**
				Thinks of consequences before doing what comes to mind.
				Puts off pleasure in order to finish necessary work.
				Follows own sense of right and wrong instead of being influenced by others.
				Puts needs and welfare of others ahead of own wishes/desires.
				Says "no" to own impulses when responsibilities must be carried out.
				Makes an effort to grow up instead of remaining immature or impulsive.
				Tries to change habits/mannerisms that bother/offend others.
				Learns from experience. Thinks about lessons learned the hard way.
				Lives by rules/spiritual principles instead of by whim/impulse.
				Accepts responsibility instead of making excuses/blaming others.
				Asks for help/advice instead of being stubborn.
				Apologizes/asks forgiveness when behavior has hurt/offended others.
				Is recognized by peers and leaders as being mature, unselfish, dependable, teachable, cooperative.
				Stops inappropriate impulses/desires before they emerge so that others will not be bothered/offended.
				Sticks to promises/agreements without being reminded or supervised.
				Goes the extra mile for others without complaining or feeling self-pity.
				Sets long-term goals and works toward them without complaining or quitting.
				Absorbs teasing/rudeness without flaring or becoming defensive.
				Is kind toward others. Avoids sarcasm/hateful remarks/putdowns.
				Resists urge to take things apart, pick at things with fingers.
				Is flexible and creative instead of being ritualized and rigid.

Add all of the scores: 0 for Never, 1 for Sometimes, 2 for Usually, 3 for Always

TOTAL SCORE _____

JORDAN EXECUTIVE FUNCTION INDEX FOR ADULTS

COUNSELOR OR TEACHER RESPONSE

Name _____   Date _____ _____ _____
                                             year   month   day

Grade _____ Retained? ___ ___   Birthdate _____ _____ _____
                           yes   no   year   month   day

If retained, what year? _____   Age   _____ _____ _____
                                               year   month   day

CLASSROOM PERFORMANCE

High Achiever	Average Achiever	Low Achiever
No Struggle	Moderate Struggle	Severe Struggle
High Motivation (always motivated)	Average Motivation (good days/bad days)	Low Motivation (seldom motivated)
Fit in well. Liked by peers. Little or no peer conflict.	Some conflict. Not always liked by peers. Could fit in with adult guidance.	Continual conflict. Disliked by peers. Could not fit in even with adult guidance.
Usually cheerful and happy.	Often moody, touchy, grouchy, irritable.	Seldom cheerful. Usually unhappy. Overly sensitive and touchy.
Outgoing. Active. Eager to cooperate. Ready to lead.	Quiet, passive. Willing to follow and cooperate.	Withdrawn. Did not want to cooperate or participate. Unconnected from group.

On the next three pages, please mark the item before each statement that is MOST like this person MOST of the time.

Never 0	Sometimes 1	Usually 2	Always 3	**ATTENTION**
				Keeps attention focused on the task without darting/drifting off on mental rabbit trails.
				Tunes out (ignores) what goes on nearby in order to keep on doing necessary tasks.
				Keeps on listening to oral information without darting/drifting off on mental rabbit trails.
				Listens to new information, understands it without saying, "Huh?" or "What?" or "What do you mean?"
				Finishes tasks without wandering off on rabbit trails before work is completed.
				Does necessary tasks without needing continual reminding and supervision.
				Can be part of a team or group without wandering off on mental rabbit trails during group activity.
				Follows the rules of games without having to be reminded.
				Can take part in group activities without being called back to attention.
				Remembers what to do after work without being reminded/supervised.
				Remembers phone messages.
				Cleans up own room/workspace without being reminded.
				Does routine chores without being reminded.
				Pays attention to TV shows/movies without wandering off on mental rabbit trails.
				Notices how others respond to his/her behavior. Picks up cues as to how own behavior should be changed.
				Notices details (how things are alike/different) without being told to notice.
				Notices how/where objects are placed and tries not to bump/knock them over.
				Notices how work pages are organized (how lines are numbered, how details are spaced, where written responses should go).
				Follows conversations without losing it or jumping to a different subject before others finish speaking.

Add all of the scores: 0 for Never, 1 for Sometimes, 2 for Usually, 3 for Always

TOTAL SCORE _____

Never 0	Sometimes 1	Usually 2	Always 3	ORGANIZATION
				Keeps track of own things without losing them.
				Gathers up things and gets them back to correct places without having to be reminded.
				Keeps track of assignments/work projects without having to be reminded/supervised.
				Keeps room/desk clean and orderly without being reminded.
				Keeps clothes/personal belongings organized without being reminded.
				Keeps work space orderly while doing tasks.
				Hears or reads instructions, then does the task in an orderly way without supervision.
				Gets things out, then puts them away without being supervised.
				Works with tools/materials, then cleans up/puts them away without being supervised.
				Spaces written work well on page without crowding or making messy.
				Plans ahead/budgets time realistically without needing reminders.
				Has realistic sense of time without needing reminding/assistance.
				Manages own money realistically without help.
				Plans activities, then explains plans to others without help.
				Plans ahead for gifts at Christmas/Hanukkah/birthdays without help.
				Notices sequence patterns (how things should be arranged) without being told.
				Keeps things together in appropriate groups (books on shelves, papers together, shoes in pairs, tools in sets, knives/forks/spoons in correct place) without being reminded/supervised.
				Keeps papers organized in notebooks, folders, files, stacks without supervision.
				Plays by the rules. Wants teammates to follow the rules.
				Does tasks in order from start to finish without skipping around.

Add all of the scores: 0 for Never, 1 for Sometimes, 2 for Usually, 3 for Always

TOTAL SCORE _____

Never 0	Sometimes 1	Usually 2	Always 3	**INHIBITION**
				Thinks of consequences before doing what comes to mind.
				Puts off pleasure in order to finish necessary work.
				Follows own sense of right and wrong instead of being influenced by others.
				Puts needs and welfare of others ahead of own wishes/desires.
				Says "no" to own impulses when responsibilities must be carried out.
				Makes an effort to grow up instead of remaining immature or impulsive.
				Tries to change habits/mannerisms that bother/offend others.
				Learns from experience. Thinks about lessons learned the hard way.
				Lives by rules/spiritual principles instead of by whim/impulse.
				Accepts responsibility instead of making excuses/blaming others.
				Asks for help/advice instead of being stubborn.
				Apologizes/asks forgiveness when behavior has hurt/offended others.
				Is recognized by peers and leaders as being mature, unselfish, dependable, teachable, cooperative.
				Stops inappropriate impulses/desires before they emerge so that others will not be bothered/offended.
				Sticks to promises/agreements without being reminded or supervised.
				Goes the extra mile for others without complaining or feeling self-pity.
				Sets long-term goals and works toward them without complaining or quitting.
				Absorbs teasing/rudeness without flaring or becoming defensive.
				Is kind toward others. Avoids sarcasm/hateful remarks/putdowns.
				Resists urge to take things apart, pick at things with fingers.
				Is flexible and creative instead of being ritualized and rigid.

Add all of the scores: 0 for Never, 1 for Sometimes, 2 for Usually, 3 for Always

TOTAL SCORE _____

JORDAN EXECUTIVE FUNCTION INDEX FOR ADULTS

SUMMARY OF BEHAVIORS

Rating Scale

0 to 11	12 to 25	26 to 40	41 to 55	56 to 60
severe	moderately severe	moderate	mild	none

FINAL SCORE · · · · · · · · · · · · · · · · · ATTENTION SUMMARY

_____ **0–11** · **Severe Attention Deficit**
Cannot function in group. Must have constant supervision to succeed. Cannot do sustained tasks without one-to-one monitoring. Cannot follow instructions without step-by-step supervision. Very short work time. Loses the task (off on rabbit trails) after 40 to 90 seconds.

Medication and diet control required before this person can function in academic, social, or work situations.

_____ **12–25** · **Moderately Severe Attention Deficit**
Can function part-time in nonacademic groups if level of stimulus is controlled. Must have continual supervision to succeed. Can work briefly (2 to 4 minutes) in sustained tasks, but reaches rapid burnout. Can follow simple one-step instructions with continual reminding and supervision. Must have one-to-one instruction to fill in gaps in skills and new information. Must be told and reminded to notice.

Medication and diet control should be considered to help this person succeed and earn praise.

_____ **26–40** · **Moderate Attention Deficit**
Can function in mainstream classroom and groups with frequent reminding/supervision. Easily distracted. Wanders off on rabbit trails and must be called back to the task. Must have frequent one-to-one help to fill gaps in skills and new information. Must be guided in following through on instructions. Notices now and then, but needs a lot of reminding to notice and pay attention.

_____ **41–55** · **Mild Attention Deficit**
Can function effectively in most situations. Occasionally becomes overly distracted by nearby events. Needs frequent monitoring to finish tasks and stay on schedules. Can be taught to monitor self and bring own attention back to task.

_____ **56–60** · **No Attention Deficit**

FINAL SCORE   ORGANIZATION SUMMARY

_____ 0–11 **Severe Organizational Deficit**
Cannot manage own things without help and supervision. Cannot remember where things are, what things are needed for certain tasks, where things were put when last used. Cannot gather up own things without supervision. Cannot remember what to take home or what to bring back to work. Loses things on bus, at home, at work. Loses clothes, books, wallet, purse, keys, important papers. Cannot recall where they were left. Leaves tools and work things in yard overnight. Cannot clean up own room without direct supervision.

Must be guided/supervised/monitored in order to finish any task. Often called "lazy" and "careless." In continual conflict with others who do not understand organizational deficits.

_____ 12–25 **Moderately Severe Organizational Deficit**
Must have supervision and help to organize. Can do better if steps are written on notes. Must be reminded to go back to notes/outlines to make sure everything has been finished. Cannot clean up own space or do chores without supervision. Cannot manage own things without being reminded. Can learn to follow checklists and outlines if others continue to remind.

Must not be expected to organize or stay on schedule without help.

_____ 26–40 **Moderate Organizational Deficit**
Ability to organize is spotty and unpredictable. Needs a lot of reminding. Responds well to written reminders (notes, outlines). Must be reminded to refer back to notes and outlines to make sure each step has been followed. Tends to be absentminded. Tends to mislay things. Keeps things in loose piles or stacks that often become mixed together. Must have help cleaning out desk/locker/work space. Has cycles of better organization/poorer organization.

_____ 41–55 **Mild Organizational Deficit**
Can develop effective strategies for staying organized and on schedule. Responds well to keeping calendars, outlines of tasks, schedules on paper. Needs to be reminded frequently. Tends to wander off on rabbit trails and forget. Appears to be absentminded and careless.

_____ 56–60 **No Organizational Deficit**

FINAL SCORE   INHIBITION SUMMARY

_____ 0–11 **Severe Problems with Self-Control**
Cannot function successfully in relationships. Severely self-focused
and self-centered. Does not notice the needs or wishes of others.
Places self first. Thinks mostly of satisfying own desires. All of personal energy goes toward fulfilling own self-needs. Does not extend
affection without demanding something in return. Cannot respond
normally to the give-and-take of friendships/family relationships/
social relationships. Is irritable, quick tempered, judgmental
when pressed to pay attention to others. Attitude is demanding,
short tempered, critical of others. Refuses to share. Demands to
be first. Wants biggest piece or share for self. Makes insatiable
demands on others. Burns others out. Is often rejected by others.
Moves from one friend to the next after short term of friendship.
Cannot share space peacefully. Usually creates conflict with
others. Cannot fit into groups. Tends to be unhappy much of the
time. Complains, gripes, finds faults when others see no problem.

This person creates continual conflicts for leaders. Must be
handled firmly. Cannot respond to normal suggestions that
depend upon noticing others. Continually argues, challenges
authority, blames others, indulges in self-pity. Uses others
without showing regret or concern.

_____ 12–26 **Moderately Severe Problems with Self-Control**
Has trouble functioning in relationships, but can do so if others
are patient and forgiving enough. Must be closely supervised in
groups. Triggers frequent arguments/conflicts with peers. Is disliked by certain leaders. Is often rejected by peers and leaders.
Can respond to coaching in how to treat others more kindly, but
such lessons do not last. Does not have a natural bent for
extending kindness and attention to others.

Leaders must intervene frequently to stop conflict or restore
peace. This person requires extra effort from leaders to keep
things going smoothly. Triggers a lot of dislike from peers. A lot
of his/her time is spent planning revenge and trying to get even.

_____ 27–41 **Moderate Problems with Self-Control**
Responds to reminding about manners and appropriate behavior.
Requires frequent one-to-one guidance in how to behave more
appropriately and less selfishly. Can respond well to reminder
cues. Responds to guidance/counseling strategies that teach this
person how to notice others. Triggers some conflict within group.
Has good days/bad days in relationships. Argues a lot over trivial
issues. Tends to split hairs over things others take in stride. Is
seldom a fully cooperative member of group. Seeks subtle ways
to get even with others.

_____ 42–55 **Mild Problems with Self-Control**
Needs frequent reminding about how to interact with others. Responds to guidance about noticing needs/wishes of others. Can learn to put own needs last or postpone wishes until later. Has good day/bad day cycles in relationships. Needs a lot of forgiveness and forgiving.

_____ 56–61 **No Problems with Self-Control**

Additional Comments or Observations

Medication

The issue of medication in the management of ADHD and ADD has always been controversial. Many fearful stories circulate about children who have been turned into "zombies" by medication to calm them down. Many parents hear stories about medication for hyperactivity blocking normal growth or adolescent development. Parents encounter all kinds of negative advice from relatives and friends when the issue of medication for the hyperactive child comes up. In my 17 years of private practice in diagnosing forms of specific learning disability, I often met parents of children such as James who were so frightened of medication that I could not refer them to medical doctors for help. Yet their lives were in chaos because of disruptive behaviors no other form of intervention had resolved.

One of the wisest voices speaking today about medication for ADHD and ADD is Edna Copeland, a psychologist who specializes in the diagnosis and treatment of attention deficits in children, adolescents, and adults. Copeland's (1991) book *Medications for Attention Disorders (ADHD/ADD) and Related Medical Problems* is outstanding in its simplicity and helpful discussions of the pros and cons of medication. As Copeland has described, there are many options for medicating patients with ADHD and ADD. She wisely points out that parents must be careful in making this kind of decision. Her book presents the consequences that will follow the child for many years if medication is not provided during critical times when the child is beyond the reach of teachers, parents, and peers.

It is often astonishing to see the positive results that medication can bring to struggling students. Figure 3.1 shows an example of the benefits of helping the brain do its work more effectively through medication. This young adult is a student in the Jones Learning Center at the University of the Ozarks. This special program helps adults who have learning disabilities earn college degrees. As Figure 3.1 shows, before using Ritalin, this student scored very low in several areas of the WAIS–R. After staying on Ritalin for several months, his performance on this intelligence test was dramatically improved. He had the same type of improvement in academic work. Without Ritalin, he struggled through high school, barely passing in spite of major tutorial help. With the help of Ritalin in college, his academic grades were dramatically better. He finished high school with a grade point average of 1.9. After taking Ritalin for a few weeks, his semester grade point average jumped to 3.2. Figure 3.1 shows the kind of improvement in learning ability we often see when medication is effectively used for persons who have ADHD and ADD.

In April 1991, I received a letter from a high school student who had read the first edition of this book:

My name is Chris. I am almost nineteen years old and still plagued by Attention Deficit Disorder since I was fourteen. For about five years, this syndrome

Wechsler Intelligence Scale Score Equivalents

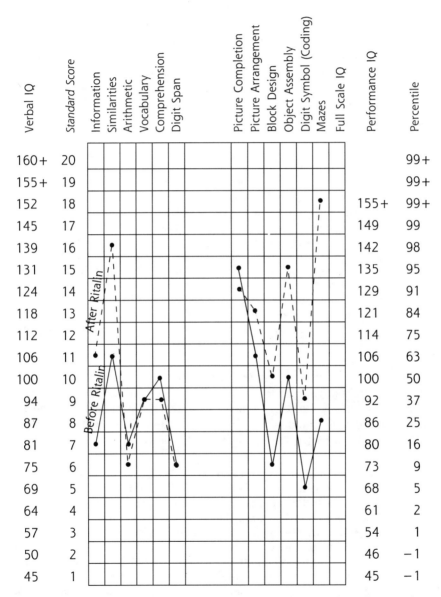

FIGURE 3.1. *Wechsler Adult Intelligence Scale–Revised* scores of a college student taking Ritalin™ for ADHD control. Solid line shows his IQ test performance without medication. Dotted line shows his improved mental ability 1 year after he started taking Ritalin.

has affected myself, my family, my friends, and my schoolwork. I cannot seem to outgrow it and I plan to attend college next fall. Please, I desprately need your help and advice. I just read one of your books on ADD syndrome but I need more information on how to cure this disorder . . .

I wrote to Chris, explaining that there is no cure for ADD. I described several medications that often help students deal more successfully with the problem. I advised him to use the checklists from Chapter 1 to pinpoint his own ADD patterns. Then I suggested that he take this information to his pediatrician who had known him all his life and ask for trial medication to help reduce his struggle. In June 1991, I received the following letter from Chris:

I have received your letter and it has helped me a great deal. There were many things I have learned in your letter about ADD. I am now taking Ritalin 30 mgs. three times a day. Now that I know the basic facts about ADD, I will try to deal with it since there is no cure. The ritalin is helping me a great deal because I have noticed that I can concentrate better on my schoolwork. I think that the military school that I attended also helped me a little bit because of the tight, structured life that I go through. In the fall I will be attending the Citadel Military College in Charleston, South Carolina. I feel that the tight structure and taking the ritalin will be my major aids in making it through college and getting a degree. For a long time I thought ADD was something little kids had, and that I was one of the very few that had it as a young adult. But after reading your book and your letter, I new see that I'm not alone and there are many others my age who share the same ordeal. I thank you very much for your help and good advice.

In Chapter 2, we met James, the "hyperactive tiger" who almost destroyed his family and himself. Although his parents could not bring themselves to try medication, many other parents of "hyperactive tigers" do try help through medication. In January 1991, I received the following letter from a mother who had read the first edition of this book:

I have just finished reading your book Attention Deficit Disorder. [I am] the parent of a 13 year old boy who was diagnosed with this disorder [with hyperactivity and conduct disorder]. . . . My son, the bright and inquisitive child that he can be (although he has a down side to that too) also devoured your book remarking that the sample of hand-writing of an ADD child could have been his. For the past two years my husband (who has also been diagnosed with ADD) and I have been in therapy while our child is being treated with the same psychologist we see and Ritalin. Two years seem like a long time, however, we all realize that our family was falling apart and we weren't sure why and bit by bit we see small improvements. I guess the major improvement here is my 13 year old who often threatened either to run away or commit suicide two years ago, doesn't anymore. With that in mind we accept the small steps we all take forward.

Earlier in this chapter, we thought about the issue of arousal as it relates to the concept of attention deficit disorder. Medication is directly related to problems of controlling arousal and finding rest. Some medications help the brain gain control over too much arousal (hyperactivity). Other medications help the brain "wake up" when there is not enough arousal to maintain a steady flow of mental energy. Edna Copeland's (1991) excellent handbook, *Medications for Attention Disorders (ADHD/ADD) and Related Medical Problems,* goes into great detail about all of the medications used to treat ADHD, ADD, Tourette's syndrome, sleep apnea, and seizure disorder. Here, we discuss only the medications most often prescribed for persons who have ADHD (too much arousal) and ADD (not enough arousal).

I follow a rather cautious approach to medication for ADHD and ADD. I offer parents and individuals this rule of thumb: *If a hyperactive or passive individual is clearly beyond the reach of leaders, teachers, or significant persons in his or her life, and if that individual clearly cannot succeed socially, educationally, and emotionally the way things are, then it is time to work with a doctor and medication.* If this individual refuses medication, then he or she will not succeed in school, at home, or in society. A person who is at the severe level of ADHD or ADD cannot function until the overaroused brain is calm or the underaroused brain is wide awake. Using the correct medication lets this happen.

The most frequently used medications for ADHD (the overaroused brain) are Ritalin and Cylert™, which are called cortical stimulants. Even though the nervous system and body activity are overcharged and hyperactive, the brain centers where learning occurs are not receiving enough blood flow and glucose in a steady stream. The synapse pathways are not sending along information regularly or smoothly. Muscle motions may be very hyperactive, but the executive functions we have studied (attention, organization, inhibition) are out of control. By itself, the brain cannot take charge of these critical functions. Adding cortical stimulants to the brain chemistry gives the central nervous system the balance it needs to take charge more effectively. Medication for ADHD and ADD "greases the pathways," as Hagerman (1983) observed, which allows mental energy to flow from start to finish without darting off on rabbit trails or becoming distracted.

Medication is like anything else we take into our bodies. Occasionally we find a person whose body chemistry is allergic to certain medication. Most ADHD and ADD persons respond to Ritalin with no allergic response. Occasionally we do find an allergic response to Ritalin. In those cases, Cylert is usually the medication prescribed. On rare occasions, certain individuals are allergic to both Ritalin and Cylert. Then we try Dexedrine™. The key to success in medication for attention deficits is to use the lowest possible dosage level. Randi Hagerman (1983), Edna Copeland (1991), Harvey Parker (1989), and other specialists have cautioned those who prescribe medication for attention deficit disorders: Academic learning improves when the dosage is kept as low as possible. If a hyperactive child becomes groggy, glassy eyed, and has trouble speaking clearly, he or she is overdosed. The body may be calm, but the learning centers in the brain are too sluggish to absorb new information. The intent of medication is not to make the muscles quiet and still; the purpose of cortical stimulants is to enable the learning centers within the brain to interconnect and process new information more effectively.

Medication is also helpful for students who are overly passive (underaroused). If cortical stimulants are not appropriate, another type of medication is often used. Ironically, these medications were originally designed to help lift individuals out of emotional depression. In our learning center at the University of the Ozarks, several adults who have ADD have responded well to imipramine, also called Tofranil™. The surface behavior is not always reliable in deciding whether imipramine or Ritalin should be used to decrease attention deficit patterns. Sometimes a person with underaroused brain functions may be hyperactive in body behavior. However, the brain pathways are too sluggish to let this hyperactive person concentrate on schoolwork. When cortical stimulants (Ritalin or Cylert) are not effective, medications such as imipramine often work well in increasing the person's ability to succeed with academic learning. Occasionally Prozac™ or Norpramin™ work effectively for adults who have ADHD or ADD. These medications are designed mainly to lift individuals out of emotional depression. They sometimes give the struggling learner the right lift to clear the thought patterns and help the student function better in school learning.

In the early 1980s, Hagerman at the Denver Children's Hospital began describing the best dosage levels of medication for children who have ADHD and ADD (Hagerman, 1983). In 1989, Parker published his Standard Ritalin Dosage Chart that followed Hagerman's earlier research. Those who work with medication for attention deficit disorders now follow certain ratios: .3 milligrams (mg) of Ritalin per kilogram (kg) of body weight for low dosage; .6 mg per kg of body weight for medium dosage; 1.0 mg per kg of body weight for high dosage. For example, a child who weighs 44 pounds (20 kg) would be given 6 mg of Ritalin for low dosage, 12 mg for a medium dosage, or 20 mg for a high dosage. Today's knowledge of adjusting dosage levels to fit the needs of the person allows physicians to make precise, safe decisions about medication for ADHD and ADD. Parents must be sure to work with a doctor who understands this kind of dosage regulation. It is critical that dosage level not be too high, or else the brain's ability to process information will be diminished.

Parents and teachers must also be aware of possible side effects of medication. If the dosage level is carefully adjusted, few persons who have ADHD or ADD experience side effects from the medication. The most commonly seen side effects of Ritalin or Cylert are loss of appetite, trouble getting to sleep, an upsetting sense of "feeling nervous," tendency to burst into tears too easily, being overly sensitive to what others say or do, and becoming constipated after starting the medication. Sometimes persons on Ritalin or Cylert develop dry mouth, the sensation of not having enough moisture in the mouth and throat. However, nobody has ever become addicted to these medications. When dosage level is correctly adjusted to fit the person's body weight, there is no danger of stunted growth or damage to hormone development during puberty. In recent years, we have learned that Ritalin can trigger moderate tic outbreaks in children who have the potential for Tourette's syndrome. In fact, Ritalin cannot be used in some patients with Tourette's syndrome. However, by working carefully to find correct dosage levels, cortical stimulant medication almost always helps persons who have ADHD or ADD.

Diet Control

In Chapter 2, we read James's story. Earlier in this chapter, we read about Phil's struggle with hypoglycemia. One of the major controversies related to attention deficit disorder is whether diet has anything to do with hyperactivity or distractibility. Numerous research studies have failed to prove that what a person eats or drinks makes a difference in how that person pays attention or performs in the classroom. Yet thousands of parents tell stories of how their youngsters react to chocolate, sugar, caffeine, or food additives. Whenever the parents of hyperactive children come together, the air is filled with stories of children's hyperactive reactions to foods, beverages, and other allergens. Those of us who work closely with those who struggle to behave, learn, and fit into their world successfully have no doubt that what certain persons eat, drink, and breathe can set them off like rockets entering orbit. William Crook (1990), Hugh Powers (1976), Ray Wunderlich (1973), and other prominent pediatricians insist that certain children have highly allergic (cytotoxic) reactions to specific food and beverage substances. During my 17 years in private practice, I saw explosive cytotoxic reactions to two generations of ADHD youngsters. Removing certain culprit foods and beverages from their diets calmed them down. Adding those culprit foods and beverages back into their diets triggered emotional and hyperactive explosions. Parents who live with "rockets in orbit" like James are desperately seeking help, regardless of what research might not have proved.

We do not know how many persons have cytotoxic reactions to what they eat, drink, or breathe. It is enough to say that many do. Based on my experience with several thousand individuals who have ADHD and ADD, certain substances come to mind when I meet a person whose behavior is out of control. My experience is that sugar is seldom the major culprit for most persons with ADHD. By itself, sugar is harmful for those who have hypoglycemia, as discussed earlier in Phil's story. In most instances, the problem comes from other things with which the sugar is combined. Many hyperactive youngsters have cytotoxic reactions to chocolate. However, it is usually the caffeine, not the sugar, in the chocolate that triggers hyperactivity. Cow's milk is a major problem for many who have ADHD. Their digestive systems are highly allergic to the ingredients in cow's milk, which quickly kicks off an inner allergic explosion. White wheat (refined wheat flour) is often a culprit that triggers hyperactive response and intestinal allergies. William Crook (1990) wrote about various forms of yeast that often trigger hyperactivity in children. I have seen explosive reactions in certain children who ate or drank products containing grape extract. Certain food dyes (Red Dye No. 2 and Yellow Dye No. 3) have been removed from our food chain because they trigger allergic responses in many people. It is not unusual to see severe allergic responses in certain persons who eat monosodium glutamate in Chinese foods. Classroom teachers tell many stories of youngsters exploding into hyperactivity after parties at school where certain sugary beverages and sweet desserts were served. The specialized discipline now called ecological psychiatry treats severely depressed and emotionally disturbed individuals by changing their diets. Careful studies are made of what each patient eats and drinks, as well as what perfumes are worn and what laundry detergents are used. Culprit foods that trigger cytotoxic responses are removed from the diet, and culprit chemicals are removed by eliminating perfumes and changing detergents. These patients invariably improve, depression decreases, and emotions come under control. It is no longer possible to contend that what persons with ADHD eat, drink, or breathe does not influence behavior. Parents of children who are severely hyperactive should seriously study the diet to find foods and beverages that may be triggering disruptive behavior.

Tight Structure

The basic problem of attention deficit disorder is that the person has no internal structure to guide him or her dependably. Thought patterns are too loose to stay on a constructive course very long. Memory is too spotty and unreliable to let rules and regulations guide the person's behavior from day to day. It is impossible for a person with ADHD or ADD to live a consistently regular, orderly life without outside help.

The greatest need faced by anyone who has ADHD or ADD is for someone else to help keep things organized and on schedule. Parents must become the source of the child's organization. Teachers must provide consistent guidelines that tell the child what to do. Any adult in a leadership position must be the eyes and ears of the person with attention deficits, especially one who is at Level 5 or higher on the severity scale. This requires extraordinary patience on the part of the adult. New mercies must be extended over and over without punishing the child for memory failure or poor organization. Adults must remember that this child cannot help being forgetful, disorganized, overly active, overly passive, or too loose to plug into his or her world successfully. Certain basic strategies must be maintained by adults if these loose thinkers are to get safely through their struggling years before they begin to outgrow the syndrome.

Chapter 1 described the incredibly poor listening comprehension we find in most children and adults who have ADHD and ADD. They seldom retain more than 30% of what they hear unless it is repeated and reinforced. The most effective way to guide a person with attention deficit disorder is to follow all oral instructions with written lists and outlines. If the person is expected to do three things, then the supervisor must make a list of those specific tasks. Each task should be numbered so the person with attention deficits has a brief visible outline:

1. Make your bed.

2. Empty the trash.

3. Feed the dog.

This kind of task outline should be posted someplace where the child will be several times during the day: on the refrigerator, on the bedroom door, on the family bulletin board, on the bathroom mirror. Then the adult consistently reminds the child," Have you done everything on your list?" This brief verbal reminder sends the child back to the list to check his or her progress. At school, teachers make lists of assignments, projects that will be due on certain dates, materials the child needs to take home, and so forth. These brief lists are taped to the child's desktop or wherever the student will spend most of the day. Again, the teacher continually reminds the child, "Joe, have you done everything on your list? Do you have all of your books gathered up to take home?" This kind of monitoring of a person who has ADHD or ADD is usually required until the middle teens. About age 14, most youngsters with attention deficits begin to remember better on their own. Some continue to need this kind of help into their late teens or early 20s. The point is that they cannot stay organized without help because their internal patterns are too loose.

It is impossible for persons who have moderate or severe ADD or ADHD to function without being supervised. Even adults who have residual attention deficits must have supervision to function successfully. Supervisors cannot walk away and leave these strugglers to carry out tasks on their own. As we saw in Chapters 1 and 2, memory patterns, sense of cause and effect, and awareness of how parts go together to make a whole are faulty in these individuals. They cannot perceive when their rooms are a mess. When their vehicles are filled with "trash," they feel right at home. They do not notice when the school desk or locker should be cleaned out. They do not notice when stuff is scattered all over the house. They cannot maintain orderly space unless they are supervised. A parent cannot expect a youngster who has ADD or ADHD to go clean up his or her room. A child or adolescent who has ADD or ADHD cannot straighten the mess in the garage unless he or she is supervised. Memory patterns are too loose and disorganized for this kind of self-directed work.

Supervisors face the task of working with the person who has attention deficits, not simply giving orders. If Pete's room is cluttered, someone else must actually be with him and show him how to put things away. If Susie's room or desk or personal space is a mess, she must have help getting it straight. The supervisor must stay right there, giving one instruction at a time. "Now, Pete, let's find all of your socks. No, Pete, leave those books alone for right now. We are looking just for socks. Don't bother about your jeans just yet. Let's keep on looking just for socks." This very specific direction guides the child in finding all of the socks. Then the supervisor guides him or her in organizing another specific item. The room is finally put in order step-by-step as the supervisor helps the loose struggler focus his or her attention on one specific object at a time. Otherwise, the person with attention deficits is distracted by everything at once.

Supervisors must remember what attention deficit disorder is. It is the inability to keep mental images clearly focused longer than a few seconds at a time. It is the inability to ignore whatever is on the edge. Thus, supervision must be provided anytime a person with ADD or ADHD is expected to carry out responsibility. This includes doing dishes, taking a bath, shampooing hair, mowing the yard, picking up dad's tools, getting home with all the necessary books for homework, getting to work on time, remembering what the boss said. Anytime a supervisor expects a person with attention deficits to follow through from start to finish, that person must be supervised to achieve success.

Several specialists who work with parents of children who have ADHD and ADD have developed excellent supervisory systems to show families how to provide structure for children like James, Jo, and Lee, whom we met earlier in this book. In 1985, Stanley Turecki wrote the thoughtful book *The Difficult Child.* This is a step-by-step approach to understanding and managing hard-to-raise children, including those like James and Jo. Turecki describes types of discipline that help frustrated parents deal more effectively with the "hyperactive tigers" that threaten to overwhelm their homes. In 1987, Russell Barkley's landmark book, *Defiant Children: A Clinician's Manual for Parent Training,* was published. Barkley teaches us how to decrease defiant behavior. He shows parents how to avoid such traps as arguing or threatening, which escalate defiance. In 1990, John Taylor published his very helpful book, *Helping Your Hyperactive Child.* Taylor offers many suggestions for developing discipline, increasing the self-esteem of children who have ADHD, and helping families adjust to the impact of children like James and Jo in the home. In

1991, Michael Gordon published his popular book, *ADHD/Hyperactivity: A Consumer's Guide for Parents and Teachers.* This easy to read book is filled with strategies that help youngsters who have ADHD succeed at home and at school. These and other guidebooks provide strategies to teach parents how to turn chaos into controlled living. Providing structure for the child who has ADHD and ADD is at the heart of these suggestions.

Allowing for Immaturity

One of the most obvious problems of attention deficit disorder is immaturity. Most individuals with ADD or ADHD are bright. In fact, a majority of these strugglers demonstrate average to superior intelligence on IQ tests if the adult giving the test knows how to work with these attentional deficits. Most students who have ADD or ADHD excel in one or two academic areas when they have enough supervision to finish assignments. Many of them are highly creative. However, they behave like much younger children.

For example, Mario is at Level 7 in ADD symptoms. He is bright with IQ 117 (Mental Age 11 years, 9 months). He is good at spelling (5th grade, 4th month level), and he is in the third month of 4th grade (Grade 4.3). Reading comprehension is excellent (7th grade, 3rd month level) when he is settled down enough to concentrate. Math skills are average at early 4th grade level. However, he acts like a 6-year-old much of the time when it comes to fitting into his class, taking his turn, sharing with others, and accepting responsibility. He fidgets, squirms, irritates his classmates, complains about having too much work to do, interrupts, and cannot stay on task without constant reminding. Mario's maturity profile would look like this:

Reading Age	12	beginning 7th grade
Mental Age	11½	middle 6th grade
Spelling Age	10½	middle 5th grade
Chronological Age	9½	middle 4th grade
Math Age	9	beginning 4th grade
Attention Span Age	7	beginning 2nd grade
Emotional Maturity Age	6½	middle 1st grade

Most adults try to work with these students backwards. Adults traditionally see how old the child is, where he or she is in school, how well the child can read, and how high the intelligence is. Adults tend to expect the child to behave and achieve on those levels. This approach does not work with youngsters such as Mario who have attention deficits. The only way to have a successful relationship with such a child is to deal with him or her the opposite way. If this bright, alert child has the attention span of a second grader, and if this 9-year-old boy has the emotional maturity of a first-grade pupil, then the adult must begin at that point. In other words, children such as Mario must be guided, nurtured, sheltered, structured, and disciplined the way adults expect to deal with a bright 6-year-old boy.

Persons of all ages who have ADD or ADHD always show this kind of spread between their highest levels of abilities and their lowest levels of maturity. If they are to find success, they must not be judged by their highest areas. They must be guided as if they were much younger. Mario's parents must structure his life the way they would if he were actually 6 years old. They must keep him out of situations that demand the emotional maturity of older children. They must not let him become involved in activities in which he will surely fail or will become overly frustrated or be regarded as a nuisance by leaders and peers. To place such a bright, sensitive, but immature boy in activities designed for 9-year-olds is to guarantee that he will be humiliated and overstressed. Adults are asking for trouble when they ignore the maturity level of youngsters who have ADD or ADHD.

The critical factor for Mario is the extreme difference between his ability to read and think and his ability to control his emotions and maintain good attention. It is usually devastating for children with this much developmental difference to be enrolled in team sports for their age group. They cannot follow coaches' instructions, they cannot remember what to do on the playing field, they cannot handle the emotional pressures of winning and losing, and they cannot be good partners in sharing and taking turns. Parents of children who have attention deficits must allow for immaturity. Most youngsters with attention deficit disorders begin to catch up in emotional maturity as puberty brings the body forward in physical development. But few are as mature as their age until their middle or late teens. When they do not outgrow these patterns (residual-type attention deficit disorder), they become adults still performing emotionally on the level of a child.

Help with Schoolwork

A major principle in working with attention deficit disorder is this: *A student with attention deficit disorder must have help with assignments.* These students are too loose, too poorly organized, and too distractible to study silently by themselves. Again, parents and teachers must keep the immaturity factor in mind. How well can a 6-year-old child study alone? How much schoolwork can a 7-year-old do without help and supervision? Until physical development is complete in the late teens or early 20s, students who have ADD or ADHD must have help to study, learn new information, prepare for tests, and finish projects. They simply cannot function academically all alone. It is counterproductive for parents to send a child with attention deficits to his or her room with orders to study for an hour.

Few students who have attention deficit disorder manage 10 good minutes of productive study out of an hour if they are alone. Most of them need a study partner at school, someone to sit nearby to answer questions, interpret instructions, and help them come back to the main track when they drift off on rabbit trails. Parents must be within touching distance as these youngsters do homework for the same reason. The only way a student who is at Level 5 or higher on the severity scale can study is to have a companion. Even if no words are exchanged, the physical presence of someone nearby helps immensely in keeping the student's attention focused on the task. If this child is alone, almost nothing is accomplished except stargazing, rabbit trailing, and time lost off in his or her world of make-believe.

Consistent Discipline

Children who have attention deficits must have discipline. This does not mean spankings or rough scoldings. Discipline for these youngsters means that supervisors maintain consistent rules and limits. A list is made of whatever the limits need to be:

1. Do not go into your sister's room without permission.

2. Do not play with Mom's or Dad's things without permission.

3. Do not ride your bike down the street without permission.

Whatever parents feel are necessary rules must be carefully explained and discussed until the child understands what the limits are. Then certain consequences must be invoked whenever the rules are broken. If Mario continues to mess with his sister's things without her permission, certain discipline will follow. If he rides his bike to forbidden areas, then certain consequences will take place. It is absolutely essential that adults maintain discipline for these youngsters who have such poor sense of organization and order. Each family must establish its own form of discipline. Ideally, a child should never be disciplined when the parent is angry. But adults cannot always do what is ideal. The goal should be that the adults be ready to invoke whatever consequences were announced ahead of time. Sometimes children who have ADD or ADHD respond best to being isolated from the rest of the family until they can calm down or think things through. Sometimes they should be grounded from doing favorite things when they break the rules. Sometimes they respond to having to do extra chores. But whatever the rules are, the child must be disciplined when he or she deliberately steps over the line. Adults must be very careful to make sure that the forgetful, loose, poorly organized child actually disobeyed rather than simply forgot. Children with attention deficits continually trespass into forbidden territory because they are too immature to read the "Keep Out" signs. But they must have enough consistent discipline to keep them out of danger and to help them learn that there are limits to be observed.

Professional Help

Parents of children who have attention deficits often must have help. A child with severe attention deficit disorder (Level 8 or 9) places enormous stress upon the marriage and all the relationships within the home and family. At times, the task of coping with ADD or ADHD is more than parents can handle alone. It is very important for parents to investigate potential professional help before becoming involved with a counselor or specialist. The least effective procedure is to judge the professional person by his or her credentials, which tell nothing about that person's effectiveness in dealing with attention deficit disorder. The most effective way for parents to find good professional help is to ask other parents. Attention deficit disorder is a common problem. In any community, there will be other families dealing with the syndrome. The most obvious strugglers are the hyperactive ones like James and Jo in Chapter 2 who attract immediate attention wherever they are. The most difficult to help are the passive ones who drift away into their private worlds of silent make-believe.

It does not take long to discover several parents who have found effective help from specific agencies. Public reputation is often the most reliable way for parents to locate help. When several parents have been helped to manage this problem successfully, word spreads quickly. Parents do need to seek fully qualified professionals, of course, but the primary concern should be how effective that professional is with attention deficit disorder. Traditional psychotherapy has very little effect on changing attention deficit. Adults must remember that this is a brain-based disorder, not simply a matter of laziness or stubbornness. The most effective professionals (counselors, pediatricians, mental health therapists) are those who view attention deficit disorder from the point of view that the central nervous system is behind schedule reaching expected maturity. The approach to helping the child with ADHD or ADD is to teach parents how to guide and discipline more effectively. Parents need to search for professional help that teaches them how to nurture children such as Mario whose intelligence is far ahead of his emotions.

Parent Organizations

One of the most disappointing and frustrating experiences of parents who have children with attention deficit disorder is to locate others who understand the disruptions going on within the home. In Chapter 2, we read of the Able family's desperation as they sought help for their son James. We followed Nate's mother as she struggled against her family's criticism toward her "weird" son. Then we met Jo Barker and shared her parent's grief over her dyslogical behavior after high school graduation. Finally, we watched Lee Hobbs's life turn around after he fell in love with a mate who could supervise their marriage. Where do parents turn to find understanding support when things at home seem to have fallen totally apart?

If a child is dyslexic, there are well-organized parent support groups such as The Learning Disabilities Association and The Orton Dyslexia Society. However, if a child struggles with ADHD and especially with ADD, national support has only recently become available. In 1985, a group of energetic parents and professionals organized a rapidly growing support group called CH.A.D.D. This group has become a powerful source of influence for legislation, as we will see in Chapter 4. CH.A.D.D. is headquartered at 499 Northwest 70th Avenue, Suite 308, Plantation, Florida 33317 (Phone: 305 587-3700), and local CH.A.D.D. groups are developing in every state. The periodic newsletter for this group, called *CH.A.D.D.ER*, is one of the most helpful publications available today. CH.A.D.D. holds annual national conferences and frequent regional seminars where the latest information about attention deficit disorders is presented. Parents of children with ADHD or ADD should by all means become involved in this support group.

4

HOPE FOR THE FUTURE AS YOUNGSTERS WITH ADHD AND ADD GROW UP

During the past 20 years, I have been dismayed by letters and calls I receive from parents after they tell their school leaders that their children have been diagnosed as having attention deficit disorder, either ADHD or ADD. Again and again, parents are told in so many words, "Well, in that case there is no use holding Elena back a year or giving her special help. After all, there is nothing you can do for ADHD or ADD. Elena will be this way all her life." This incredible misperception exists at all levels of American education, from preschool workers to professors at major universities. It is always a shock to hear this kind of report from bewildered parents who have finally received a meaningful explanation for a child's difficult behavior. To be told by school leaders that

Elena is in effect doomed to be this way all her life is more than most parents can endure. I continually hear the question from grieving, often angry parents: "Is there no hope for our child? Will Elena always be this way?"

As we have seen earlier in this book, certainly there is hope for persons who have ADHD or ADD. Even when there is violent behavior, as we found in James, or irresponsibility, as we read in Jo's story, there is hope. Parents may not always find the "cure" they pray to discover, but there is hope if certain steps are followed. In Chapters 2 and 3, we read about the hope the Able family found through strict diet control for their "hyperactive tiger" James. After being battered for the first 9 years of the boy's life, they found hope and at least partial relief. Now he is in college working toward a specialty in psychology. The Barkers found less hope as Jo broke their hearts following high school graduation. As we finished her story in Chapter 2, we did not leave her frustrated parents in a state of happiness. But as we shall see later in this chapter, there is hope for the Jos of the future as new knowledge of brain structure and body chemistry is acquired in the near future. In Chapter 3, we met Phil who had lost his wife and children and who had never finished anything in his life. Yet Phil's story contained a great deal of hope because solutions to his problems were at his fingertips, ready to be taken. Nate and his mother found hope through medication that helped him become better organized and brave enough to lay his doll Roy aside. Lee found hope, as his mother wrote in her book, when he met a partner whom he could trust. Together, they built a marriage relationship that enabled him to thrive because she could be his supervisor. Yes, there is hope for those who have attention deficit disorders. This hope comes through several sources if families are patient enough and courageous enough to keep on seeking until help is found.

Late Bloomers Finally Catch Up

It seems so obvious, yet we overlook this fact so easily: Not all of us grow up on the same developmental schedule. We are often in awe of early bloomers who shoot out ahead of peers in height, weight, sexual maturity, and achievement. Recently, the middle school choir at the church my wife and I attend presented a delightful musical with costumes and sets they had constructed. As this chorus of youngsters took their places, my wife and I were amazed at the extreme differences in physical development we saw in those children. They ranged in age from 11 to 13. One 11-year-old girl towered head and shoulders above all the others; two very small 11-year-olds were only slightly taller than her belt buckle. One 12-year-old boy already had a deep voice that boomed off key when he tried to sing softly. Two 13-year-old boys still had soprano voices without a trace of puberty setting in. Here was a striking visual lesson in the differences we take for granted in our children. Yet when it comes to academic performance, we assume that all students who are the same age are also the same in scholastic abilities.

One frequent earmark of those who have attention deficits is late physical maturation. In Chapter 1, we reviewed the shoestring baby syndrome. These late bloomers remain behind typical growth schedule until they reach their early adult years. They are low weight infants who often struggle with underdeveloped digestive systems. Their immune systems cannot fight off infections and allergies during their early years. Tooth development is usually late, with baby teeth not shed until age 7 or later, and front permanent teeth are seldom fully in before age 8 or older. They are too immature to handle mainstream classwork successfully the first several years of school. They behave like much younger children even after they enter high school. Hormone production that starts the cycles of puberty and adolescence is usually quite late. These late bloomers seldom have the physical and sexual maturity of their agemates. They are rarely mature enough at age 16 to drive the family car safely on their own. They are not ready to begin practicing romance when their classmates are going out on dates. They are usually well into their early 20s before they have the social maturity we expect to see in teenage students. Eventually, however, most of these late bloomers blossom into marvelous individuals as they leave those first 22 years of struggle behind them.

While late bloomers are lagging behind, it is not always easy to think of hope. When they embarrass themselves and their friends and families, it is hard to hope that they will ever become more mature. When they display the emotional habits of much younger persons, it is hard for parents to feel pride in these youngsters who "just won't try to grow up." When these late bloomers prefer to play with little kids instead of enjoying their own age group, parents feel exasperated and often desperate. But late bloomers begin to mature at certain stages. About age 14, teachers and parents begin to notice significant changes. As these late bloomers enter high school, they may still be far less physically mature than their peers, but they usually begin to need less supervision. They begin to respond better to notes, phone reminders, and daily schedules. They begin to take more interest in their appearance. They begin to want to grow up, in sharp contrast to previous years when they really did not care. About age 16, these late developers begin to show still further maturity in their grooming, memory for details, staying on schedules with less reminding required, more responsibility with less forgetting, and better performance in academic work along with better study habits. By age 18, these late bloomers have caught up with most 16-year-olds, which is a giant step forward in closing the gaps that used to drive their parents nuts. The real breakthrough for late bloomers comes in the early 20s. In most cases, age 22 is the breakthrough year. Sometimes maturation does not occur until age

24 or later. Occasionally the blooming does not happen until age 30 or even older. But most individuals who have attention deficit disorder during childhood experience this kind of catching up.

There is hope if families are patient and learn how to wait. Even dreadfully difficult persons like Jo begin to mellow about age 30. Unless mental illness emerges, as it often does in certain fragile people who had ADHD or severe ADD during childhood, adult years bring radiant hope to fulfillment. It is tragic when well-meaning leaders say to parents of a child who has ADHD or ADD, ''There is nothing you can do. Elena will be this way all her life.'' For those of us who have seen two or three generations of late bloomers grow up, this is ignorant nonsense. As I work with the children and now the grandchildren of the first strugglers I knew many years ago, I clearly see the joyous hope if leaders are wise enough to show families how to see it.

Medication and Diet Control

In Chapter 3, we reviewed the most helpful medications available that enable persons with ADHD and ADD to process information more successfully. As Edna Copeland (1991) has shown in her remarkable manual, *Medications for Attention Disorders,* physicians are becoming increasingly skilled in adjusting dosage levels to fit the differences of individual body chemistries. As more becomes known about brain structure through positron emission tomography (PET), magnetic resonance imaging (MRI), brain electrical activity mapping (BEAM), and other brain imaging techniques, the science of medication for attention deficits will become even more helpful. Instead of having only a handful of effective medications from which to choose, by the turn of this century we will have a wide variety of medications designed to adjust neuronal functions as well as we can fine-tune a musical instrument. We have seen the devastating effects upon behavior and emotional control when allergic reactions are triggered by cytotoxic substances in foods, beverages, and the air we breathe. We are gradually cleaning up our environment. Little by little, contamination is being eliminated. We are making similar progress in taking culprit ingredients out of our food chain. Persons who have ADHD are finding it easier to avoid triggering food substances. Federal regulations are forcing manufacturers to print details of food ingredients on the labels. This trend will continue, making it easier for individuals and families to avoid explosive reactions to what they eat, drink, or breathe. Within a few more years, newer medications and more carefully controlled food production will give parents hope of bringing severely hyperactive children under control.

Civil Rights Protection

In the early 1970s, the federal government began to make sure that handicapped persons would not be discriminated against in education and in society as a whole. In 1973, the Rehabilitation Act of 1973 was passed by Congress. Section 504 of Public Law (PL) 93-112 spelled out the ways in which local, state, and national agencies should meet the needs of persons with handicaps. Section 504 was the first government effort to see that learning disabilities were recognized and treated by educators. As PL 93-112 was implemented, the emphasis of meeting special needs became focused upon persons with physical handicaps that interfered with work, getting about, or caring for themselves. Groups of parents of struggling learners began to organize in order to press national leaders to meet the special educational needs of students who had learning difficulties. Out of that parent movement grew the highly effective group then called the Association for Children with Learning Disabilities (ACLD). Today this group is called the Learning Disabilities Association (LDA). By 1975, the ACLD and other groups encouraged Congress to pass new legislation specifically for the benefit of students who had learning disabilities, including dyslexia and attention deficit disorders. Thus, PL 94-142, the Education of the Handicapped Act, came into effect. For more than a decade, this law mandated how each school district in the United States would meet the needs of students who were diagnosed as having specific learning disability.

These early efforts to make sure that all persons who have learning disabilities were educated appropriately were not perfect, to be sure. Many parents were forced to file litigation against schools to obtain appropriate educational help for their children. Several cases made their way to the Supreme Court before it was made clear what schools must do for struggling learners. In 1990, further legislation was passed by Congress regarding the special needs of students with learning differences. This new legislation is called Individuals with Disabilities Education Act (IDEA). This legislation is an effort to change the older concept that persons who have learning disabilities are not necessarily handicapped. Along with the 1990 revision of PL 94-142 has come the movement by many leaders to discontinue the term "learning disability" in favor of "learning difference."

Still further federal help is on the way for persons who have disabilities or handicaps. In July 1992, a new body of legislation will take effect. Public Law 101-336, the Americans with Disabilities Act of 1990 (ADA), will regulate how employers shall treat persons who have physical limitations, as well as those who are dyslexic or have attention deficit disorders (ADHD or ADD). As today's children grow up, both IDEA and ADA will protect their civil rights and help to ensure that their educational and employment needs will be met without discrimination. Through forward-looking legislation, there is a great deal of hope for those who struggle to find their place in the classroom, on the job, and in society.

Better Diagnosis

Countless parents have faced the heartbreak of poor diagnosis. Earlier in this book we read of families who struggled to find the reasons for their children's behavior. Almost daily I receive mail or calls from parents asking the critical question, "Where can we go to have our child's problem diagnosed? Our pediatrician does not have the answer. We can't find anyone in our community who can help us. Where can we go for the right kind of help?" Diagnosing ADHD and ADD is not always easy, and once a diagnosis is made, helping the child or adult find relief from the symptoms is not always simple. This is especially true if the criteria learning disability standard of score discrepancy is the only diagnostic method used. It takes a keen professional eye with much intuitive insight to see all of the strands that make up the fabric of attention deficit disorder. This is particularly true if the child has panic attacks, goes into phobic reactions as James did when he saw inflated balloons, hides behind make-believe as Nate did with his doll Roy, has strong cytotoxic reactions to foods or beverages, has hypoglycemic reaction to certain foods, or "blinks" in and out as Jim Reisinger described in Chapter 1. If the child who has ADHD or ADD is also dyslexic, the strands are even harder to unravel. And if the child has poor central vision so that he or she cannot keep print in focus long enough to read a page, it becomes increasingly difficult to make a correct diagnosis. In addition, certain youngsters who display signs of attention deficit disorder also begin to slip into the neurotic twilight zone of borderline mental illness as puberty begins. Making a correct diagnosis of ADHD or ADD is seldom as simple as it may seem.

Yet there is much hope as we near the close of this century. Brain imaging research is rapidly making precise diagnosis of brain functions available to us all. Earlier we reviewed Martha Denckla's MRI studies of the cerebellum that led to the *Jordan Executive Function Index.* PET studies by Frank Wood (1991) and other specialists have revealed areas of slow blood flow that contributes to ADHD and ADD. Alan Zametkin et al.'s brain studies of glucose metabolism (see Figure 1.1) have pinpointed specific causes for ADHD. As this kind of knowledge grows about how the living brain functions, a new generation of diagnosticians will learn how to separate the different strands within the tangled fabric of learning disability, or learning difference. When James, Nate, Lee, and even Jo become parents in the next decade, they will find much hope through better diagnosis and treatment of their children, who likely will follow the patterns we have seen in their moms and dads.

References

American Psychiatric Association. (1980). *Diagnostic and statistical manual of mental disorders* (3rd ed.). Washington, DC: Author.

American Psychiatric Association. (1987). *Diagnostic and statistical manual of mental disorders* (3rd ed., rev.). Washington, DC: Author.

Anastopoulos, A. D., & Barkley, R. A. (1991). Biological factors in attention deficit-hyperactive disorder. *CH.A.D.D.ER, 5,* 1.

Barkley, R. A. (1987). *Defiant children: A clinician's manual for parent training.* New York: Guilford.

Clements, S. D. (1966). *Minimal brain dysfunction in children* [Monograph No. 3, U.S. Department of H.E.W., Public Health Service Bulletin No. 1415], NINDS, Washington, DC.

Copeland, E. D. (1991). *Medications for attention disorders (ADHD/ADD) and related medical problems.* Atlanta: SPI Press.

Crook, W. G. (1990). *Help for the hyperactive child.* Jackson, TN: International Foundation.

Denckla, M. (1991, February 25). *Brain behavior insights through imaging.* Paper presented at the Learning Disabilities Association National Conference, Chicago, IL.

Gordon, M. (1991). *ADHD/hyperactivity: A consumer's guide for parents and teachers.* DeWitt, NY: GSI Publications.

Hagerman, R. J. (1983, March 8). *Developmental pediatrics.* Paper presented at the New Frontiers Symposium, Steamboat Springs, CO.

Harvard Medical School. (1985). Attention deficit disorder. *Mental Health Letter, 2*(3), 1.

Hoffer, E. (1982). *Between the devil and the dragon.* New York: Harper & Row.

Jordan, D. R. (1988). *Jordan prescriptive/tutorial reading program.* Austin, TX: PRO-ED.

Jordan, D. R. (1989). *Overcoming dyslexia in children, adolescents, and adults.* Austin, TX: PRO-ED.

Jordan, D. R. (1991). Whatever happened to ADD without hyperactivity? *CH.A.D.D.ER, 4,* 4.

Parker, H. C. (1989). *The ADD hyperactivity workbook for parents, teachers, and kids.* Plantation, FL: Impact Publications.

Powers, H. W. S., Jr. (1976). Dietary measures to improve behavior and achievement. *Academic Therapy, 9*(3), 12–31.

Silver, L. (1991, February 27). *Attention deficit–hyperactivity disorder: If it is for real, why all of the confusion?* Paper presented at the Learning Disabilities Association National Conference, Chicago, IL.

Taylor, J. F. (1990). *Helping your hyperactive child.* New York: Prima.

Turecki, S. (1985). *The difficult child.* New York: Bantam Books.

von Hilshimer, G. (1974). *Allergy, toxins, and the learning disabled child.* Novato, CA: Academic Therapy.

Weis, G., & Hechtman, L. T. (1986). *Hyperactive children grown up.* New York: Guilford.

Wender, P. H. (1987). *The hyperactive child, adolescent, and adult: Attention deficit disorder through the lifespan.* New York: Oxford.

Wood, F. (1991, February 25). *Brain imaging, learning disabilities.* Paper presented at the Learning Disabilities Association National Conference, Chicago, IL.

Wunderlich, R. C., Jr. (1973). *Allergy, brains, and children coping.* St. Petersburg, FL: Johnny Reads.

Zametkin, A. (1991). The neurobiology of attention-deficit hyperactivity disorder. *CH.A.D.D.ER, 5,* 1.

Zametkin, A. J., Nordahl, T. E., Gross, M., King, A. C., Semple, W. E., Rumsey, J., Hamburger, S., & Cohen, R. M. (1990). Cerebral glucose metabolism in adults with hyperactivity of childhood onset. *New England Journal of Medicine, 323,* 1361–1367.

Index